Martin Buber and the Eternal

Martin Buber and the Eternal

Maurice Friedman, Ph.D.

**Professor of Philosophy, Religious Studies,
and Comparative Literature,
San Diego State University**

 **HUMAN SCIENCES PRESS, INC.**
72 FIFTH AVENUE
NEW YORK, N.Y. 10011

Copyright © 1986 by Maurice Friedman.
Published by Human Sciences Press, Inc.
72 Fifth Avenue, New York, New York 10011

Printed in the United States of America
987654321

Library of Congress Cataloging-in-Publication Data

Friedman, Maurice S.
  Martin Buber and the eternal.

  Includes index.
  1. Buber, Martin, 1878–1965—Contributions in
philosophy of religion. 2. Religion—Philosophy—
History—20th century. I. Title.
B3213.B84F68   1986   200′.1   85-27283
ISBN 0-89885-284-6

To Virginia

who has helped confirm in my life
that "all real living is meeting"

Contents

Preface

After the completion of my monumental 3-volume biography of Martin Buber,[1] I am myself somewhat surprised to be bringing forth still another "Buber book." I had originally thought of incorporating the material in this little book into *The Human Way*.[2] My later intention was to make it an integral part of *You Are My Witnesses*.[3] Finally, it became clear to me that it should stand as a statement of its own on Martin Buber's philosophy of religion as I have plumbed and engaged it in the course of more than 35 years of work on Buber's life and thought. If it is the shortest of the 15 books that I have written, it is also in some ways the most concise. Although a number of the nine chapters were published earlier in some form or other, it is by no means a collection of essays. On the contrary, it comes together in a gestalt, an integral statement of my understanding of Buber's philosophy of religion and its implications for ethics, the history of religion, interreligious dialogue, and religious education. As such, it should be of interest to a broad range of readers from many fields of study and thought and from many religions.

Much of Chapter 2—"Biblical Existentialism: Creation, Revelation, Redemption"—was published earlier under the title "Martin Buber's Challenge to Jewish Philosophy" in the July 1965 issue of *Judaism*. Chapter 3 was published in slightly different form under the title "Revelation and Reason in Martin Buber's Philosophy of Religion" in the Winter 1971 issue of the *Bucknell Review*. Chapters 4 and 5 were originally combined as "The Bases of Buber's Ethics" in *The Philosophy of Martin Buber*, edited by Paul

Arthur Schilpp and myself (German 1963, English 1967, Japanese 1971). Chapter 6 was published under the title "Martin Buber's Approach to Comparative Religion" in Jochanan Bloch, Haim Gordon, and Menachem Dorman, editors, *Martin Buber: A Centenary Volume* (Hebrew 1981, German 1983, English 1984). Chapter 7 was originally published under the title "Martin Buber and Asia" in the Fall 1976 issue of *Philosophy East and West* and as "Martin Buber's Dialogue with Oriental Philosophy" in Nathan Katz, editor, *Buddhism and Western Philosophy* (1981). Chapter 8 was originally published under the title "Martin Buber's 'Theology' and Religious Education" in the January–February 1959 issue of *Religious Education*. The Appendix was originally published under the title "Dialectical Faith versus Dialogical Trust" in the May 1971 issue of *The Eastern Buddhist*. Chapters 1 and 9 were written especially for this book. I wish to acknowledge receiving permissions for these from *Judaism,* Associated University Presses, Open Court, Haim Gordon, *Philosophy East and West, Religious Education,* and The Eastern Buddhist Society respectively.

A special word is due my inclusion in this book of my response to Stanley Romaine Hopper's essay "Eclipse of God and Existential Mistrust" as an "Appendix." Being a reply, it does not constitute a chapter proper, and is rather of interest to the philosopher and the scholar of religion than to the educated laypeople who may find themselves drawn to the other parts of this book. The interest it will have for the professional philosopher or scholar is not, of course, Professor Hopper's essay itself, which cannot be reprinted here, nor even his thought for its own sake, however valuable that may be. Martin Buber's philosophy of religion is of a deceptive simplicity. That might lead one to suppose that it is not likely to be misunderstood. The very opposite is the case. Martin Buber once remarked to me that the essays devoted to the different aspects of his thought in *The Philosophy of Martin Buber* volume of *The Library of Living Philosophers* represented the whole range of possible misunderstandings. Stanley Hopper's essay is an excellent example of such misunderstandings on the part of a highly qualified scholar and thinker.

For this reason my response may serve to sharpen the grasp of Buber's philosophy of religion for those who are given to a dialectical turn of mind and who enjoy the give and take of critical argument. This is particularly so because Hopper's essay focuses on those very aspects of Buber's philosophy of religion that I have discussed in Chapter 9—the eclipse of God and existential trust and mistrust. It is also so because Hopper's misunderstanding of Buber's philosophy of religion in general, and of the Eternal Thou and Buber's approach to religious symbolism and to dialogical knowledge in particular, give me the occasion to illuminate further these aspects of Buber's thought. Finally it is so because Hopper himself puts forward and to some extent embodies two of the very modern philosophies that Buber has criticized as contributing to the eclipse of God—that of Martin Heidegger and that of C. G. Jung. It is *not* my purpose to disparage Professor Hopper himself, who is justly renowned for his contribution to religious thought and literature. I hope he will forgive my using him as a springboard for the further clarification of Buber's philosophy of religion.

I am grateful to my friend Virginia Shabatay, to whom this book is dedicated, for helpful suggestions—particularly her call for a considerable expansion of Chapter 9 to include some of the more positive and hopeful things Buber had to say!

Maurice Friedman

1

Dialogue and the "Eternal Thou"

Strictly speaking, Martin Buber has no philosophy of religion. What he says of Hasidism is true of his own "philosophy of dialogue": it does not wish to instruct us about God's nature but to show us the road on which we can meet God. Martin Buber is not concerned with the word about God but the Word of God, more exactly, with the word that points to our relation to the God whom we can never know as he is in himself apart from that relation.

"God," says Buber in his classic work *I and Thou,* "is the Being that is directly, most nearly, and lastingly, over against us, that may properly only be addressed and not expressed." God is the "Absolute Person" who is met whenever we meet our fellow man or the world as "Thou." He is the "eternal Thou" who cannot become an "It." The true God can never be an object of our thought, not even the "Absolute" object from which all others derive. We do not *discover* God, therefore; we *respond* to him. We become aware of the address of God in everything that we meet if we remain open to that address and ready to respond with our whole being. God wants to come into the world through our loving relation with the people we live with and meet, the animals that help us with our farm-work, the soil we till, the materials we shape, the tools we use. "Meet the world with the fullness of your being and you shall meet Him," writes Buber. "If you wish to be-lieve, love!"

Religion and Philosophy

Does this mean that the objective content of religion does not matter? Far from it. Yet it matters only as it points back to our relation with God rather than as it seeks to take its place. Basically, religion is not philosophy, which seeks to know the absolute as an object of contemplation; it is a knowing which takes place within the dialogue itself and cannot be detached from it. Religious knowledge is "mu-tual contact. . . . the genuinely reciprocal meeting in the fullness of life between one active existence and another," and faith is entering into this reciprocity, binding oneself in relationship "with an undemonstrable and unprovable, yet even so, in relationship, knowable Being, from whom all meaning comes."

The religious essence of every religion is found, says Buber, in "the certainty that the meaning of existence is open and accessible in the actual lived concrete, not above the struggle with reality but in it." This meaning won "in the unreduced immediacy of the moment" must be con-firmed in one's life, verified and authenticated by one's own commitment and response. This is why religious real-ity begins with what biblical religion calls the "fear of God." "It comes when our existence between birth and death becomes incomprehensible and uncanny, when all security is shattered through . . . the essential mystery."

The believing person passes through this dark gate into the everyday, ready now to live with the mystery. "Directed and assigned to the concrete, contextual situations of his existence. . . . he endures in the face of God the reality of lived life, dreadful and incomprehensible though it be."[1] Philosophizing and philosophy, in contrast, begin ever anew with one's definitely looking away from his concrete situation, hence with the primary act of abstraction.

Buber's understanding of religion and philosophy corresponds to the two complementary, and at the same time opposing, relationships that he designates as the basic modes of human existence—"I-Thou" and "I-It." "For man the existent is either face-to-face being or passive object" (Gegenüber oder Gegenstand). *Either* it is the direct, reciprocal, present relationship of two persons each of whom enters the relationship with the whole of his person, or even the faithful, if not fully reciprocal, relationship of one person with the nonhuman reality over against one—a tree, a cat, a symphony. *Or* existence is the indirect, nonreciprocal, essentially already categorized and fixed relationship of active knowing and using subject to passive, known, and used object. Without the "I-It" we could not live, for through it we order our world and build our economies. Yet if we live in this relationship alone, we are not truly human. I become a person, an "I," through being called into existence in an "I-Thou" relationship and through responding to this call. "I-Thou" again becomes "I-It" for me, but this It can be taken up and interpenetrated by the Thou, and it is through this ever-renewed act of entering into reciprocal relation that I authenticate my humanity.

Religion and philosophy represent the highest stages of these two modes of existence whose interchange makes up our human life:

I-Thou finds its highest intensity and transfiguration in religious reality, in which unlimited Being becomes, as absolute person, my partner. I-It finds its highest concentration and illumination in philosophical knowledge. In this knowledge the extraction of the subject from the I of the immediate lived togetherness of I and It and the transformation of the It into the object detached in its essence produces the exact thinking of contemplated existing beings, yes, of contemplated Being itself.[2]

Human Truth and Religious Symbols

But the real opposition for Buber is not between religion and philosophy. It is between that philosophy which sees the absolute in universals and hence removes reality into the systematic and the abstract, and that which means the bond of the absolute with the particular and hence points us back to the reality of the lived concrete—to the immediacy of real meeting with the beings over against us.

Human truth is participation in Being, writes Buber, not conformity between a proposition and that to which the proposition refers. It cannot claim universal validity, yet it can be exemplified and symbolized in actual life.

Any genuine human life-relationship to Divine Being—i.e., any such relationship effected with a man's whole being—is a human truth, and man has no other truth. The ultimate truth is one, but it is given to man only as it enters, reflected as in a prism, into the true life-relationships of the human person.[3]

The religious reality of the meeting with God knows no image of God, nothing comprehensible as object. "It knows only the Presence of the Present One. Symbols of Him, whether images or ideas, always exist first when and insofar as Thou becomes He, and that means It." Yet God, "so we may surmise," suffers that one look at him through these necessarily untrue images—until they claim to be more than signs and pointers to him, until "they swell themselves up and obstruct the way to Him, and He removes Himself from them." At this point the philosopher's criticism of the image and the God which it symbolizes arouses the religious person who destroys the images that manifestly no longer do justice to God and "sets forth right across the God-deprived reality to a new meeting" with the nameless Meeter.[4]

For Buber, in total consonance with Jewish tradition, the action of creation goes on incessantly; for God incessantly calls man and the world into being. Man is the completer of God's creation and the initator of his redemption. He has real independence, accordingly, and "takes part with full freedom and spontaneity" in the dialogue with God that forms the essence of his existence. But he must enter this dialogue with his whole being. He must bring every aspect of his existence into it. He cannot allow any sphere of his life to remain separate from God; for God claims the whole of his personal existence—his social and political life as well as his private relations, his inner intentions as well as his outer acts. The Holy is not a separate and secluded sphere of being. It is open to all spheres of being and it is that through which they find their fulfillment. Man lets God into the world through living a true life "here where he stands," through satisfying "the claim of situations out of deep readiness to respond with his whole life, and in such a way that the sum of his actions and attitudes expresses at the same time the unity of his being in its willingness to accept responsibility."[5] Only in such responsibility does the soul achieve unification, and, conversely, only as a whole being can a person attain the fullness of dialogue.

Only, too, through the wholeness of the person in fullness of response does the person become aware of his or her personal direction—the special way to God that he or she can realize in his or her relations with the world and other human beings. Every person in the world represents a created uniqueness given not for mere existence but for the fulfillment of a purpose that only he or she can fulfill. "The humanly right is ever the service of the single person who realizes the right uniqueness purposed for him in his creation."[6] One experiences one's uniqueness as a designed or performed one, intrusted to one for execution; yet everything that affects one participates in this execution. Although "the one direction of the hour towards God . . . changes time and again by concretion," each moment's new direction is *the* direction if reality is met in lived concreteness. Buber's "direction" is thus of crucial significance for his philosophy of religion, which is a philosophy of the relationship between the "I" of the human being and the "eternal Thou" that is met in every finite Thou, the Thou in which the parallel lines of relation intersect.

2

Biblical Existentialism

Creation, Revelation, Redemption

Judaism as the Source for Buber's Philosophy

Martin Buber's philosophy does not fit the traditional form of systematic philosophy. Still less does it fit that tradition which approaches Judaism from the standpoint of some philosophy entirely independent of it, such as the Platonism of Philo Judaeus, the Aristotelianism of Maimonides, or the Neo-Kantianism of Hermann Cohen. In its philosophical approach Buber's philosophy is more firmly moored in Jewish sources than any of these, more so even than the existentialism of his friend Franz Rosenzweig, whose *Star of Redemption* still bears in its method the stamp of the Hegelian dialectic even while it rejects its content. In his suggestion that Buber has read his existentialist philosophy into his interpretation of Hasidism, Gershom Scholem implies that Buber has applied a philosophy of an entirely alien origin to the elucidation of the contents of Judaism. In fact, Buber's general philosophy develops from the beginning in clear interaction with his philosophy and interpretation of Judaism.

In *Martin Buber: The Life of Dialogue* I point to "the dialogue that has existed throughout Buber's creative life between Buber as original thinker and Buber as interpreter of tradition. Here, too," I suggest, "one must walk the 'narrow ridge'—between the temptation of considering Buber a thinker who reads his philosophy into his interpretations and that of considering him a thinker who derives his philosophy from his religious tradition." What took place rather was a fruitful dialelctic in which "every important step forward in the development of Buber's philosophy is reflected in his philosophy of Judaism.

> His existentialism, his philosophy of community, his religious socialism, and his dialogical philosophy all develop within his philosophy of Judaism as well as outside of it. There is, thus, an essential unity of what are in Buber's writings two separate streams of developing thought.[1]

When we consider Buber's Jewish existentialism, therefore, we must not allow the term "existentialism" to lead us to overlook the fact that both the content and the approach of Buber's philosophy have Jewish roots. This does not mean that they necessarily represent the whole of Judaism in balanced fashion. On the contrary, they reflect a good deal more of biblical and Hasidic Judaism than they do of Talmudic Judaism, medieval Jewish philosophy, or modern liberal Judaism. But the principle of selection is no arbitrary one, nor is it one imported from some worldview entirely foreign to Judaism.

The Biblical Emuna

At the center of Buber's existentialism stands the biblical *emuna*—the unconditional trust in the relationship with

God. This is the "holy insecurity" which is willing to go out to meet the unique present, the "narrow ridge" which realizes the unity of the contraries in action and grace, freedom and binding. This trust expresses itself in Buber's statements that "all real living is meeting," that meaning is open and accessible in the "lived concrete," that transcendence addresses us in the events of everyday life, that man's true concern is not *gnosis*—unravelling the divine mysteries—but *devotio*—the way of man in partnership with God. Although Paul Tillich accepts Buber's interpretation of biblical faith as an I-Thou relationship, he believes that one must finally go beyond God as Thou to the Ground of Being, the "God above God." To this extent he attempts to shore up the biblical *emuna* with the *gnosis* that takes refuge in comprehensive concepts. For Buber, in contrast, one cannot go beyond the meeting with the "Absolute Person" whose personality is not his nature but his relationship with us. We know God only in relationship; we cannot know him as he is "in himself." Like the imageless God of the Hebrew Bible, Buber's "eternal Thou" means the ever-renewed meeting with the God Who will be there *as* he will be there.

The only gate which leads to the Bible as a reality, writes Buber, is the faithful distinction between creation, revelation, and redemption, not as "manifestations of God, but as stages, actions, and events in the course of His intercourse with the world." Franz Rosenzweig, in his *Star of Redemption,* Buber adds, "has the great merit of having shown this to our era in a new light." Not only Buber's interpretation of biblical Judaism but also his philosophy in general is informed and illuminated to a remarkable extent by these three "stages, actions, and events" in the course of God's intercourse with the world.

Nothing is more central to Buber's "I-Thou" philosophy than his understanding of creation. It is creation in the biblical sense that underlies Buber's assertion that man is given a ground on which to stand and that he is able to go out to meet God, man, and world from that ground. It is creation which informs Buber's belief in man's spontaneity and freedom that cannot be modified by any original sin and in man's responsibility that cannot be abridged by any fate. This approach to creation is also inherent in Buber's understanding of God as the Absolute Person, who *is* not a person but *becomes* one, so to speak, to love and be loved, to know and be known by us. This is the paradox of the God who remains unlimited and yet enters into direct relation with us.

> That you need God more than anything, you know always in your heart. But do you not also know that God needs you, in the fullness of his eternity, you? How would there be the human being if God did not need it, and how would there be you? You need God in order to be, and God needs you—for just that which is the meaning of your life. Teachings and poetry take pains to say more, and they say too much: what murky and overweening talk that is of "the God that becomes"—but there is a becoming of the God that is, that we know unswervingly in our hearts. The world is not divine play, it is divine destiny. That the world, that man, that the human person, that you and I exist, has divine meaning.
>
> Creation—it happens in us, it burns into us, burns around us, we tremble and faint, we surrender. Creation—we take part in it, we meet the Creator, reach out to him, helpers and comrades.[2]

This paradox sets Buber in contrast to traditional metaphysics which demands the choice between an absolute that is not in relation to the world and a God who is in relation and therefore less than absolute. It is this that led the eminent Whiteheadian metaphysician Charles Hartshorne to speak of Buber as no metaphysician and at the same time one of the greatest metaphysicians, and it is this, too, that led Buber to reply that he and Hartshorne could only agree on the first of those two propositions!

Creation Is the Road

Buber's essentially Jewish approach to creation illuminates his differences from one of the most important Christian existentialists of modern times—Søren Kierkegaard. When Buber complains in "The Question to the Single One" that Kierkegaard reaches God by subtracting the world, he is criticizing Kierkegaard's tendency to remove God from an essential relationship to creation.

"In order to come to love," says Kierkegaard about his renunciation of Regina Olsen, "I had to remove the object." That is sublimely to misunderstand God. Creation is not a hurdle on the road to God, it is the road itself. We are created along with one another and directed to a life with one another. Creatures are placed in my way so that I, their fellow-creature, by means of them and with them find the way to God. A God reached by their exclusion would not be the God of all lives in whom all life is fulfilled. A God in whom only the parallel lines of single approaches intersect is more akin to the "God of the philosophers" than to the "God of Abraham and Isaac and Jacob." God wants us to come to him by means of the Reginas he has created and not by renunciation of them. . . . The real God lets no shorter line reach him than each man's longest, which is the line embracing the world that is accessible to this man.[3]

This same attitude toward creation underlies Buber's criticism in "Education" of the teacher who follows the principle of Eros, or choice through inclination, in contrast to the true teacher who "finds his pupil there before him."

From this unerotic situation the *greatness* of the modern educator is to be seen—and most clearly when he is a teacher. He enters the school-room for the first time, he sees them crouching at the desks, indiscriminately flung together, the misshapen and the well-proportioned, animal faces, empty faces, and noble faces in indiscriminate confusion, like the presence of the created universe; the glance of the educator accepts and receives them all . . . he seems to me to be a representative of the true God. For if God "forms the light and creates darkness," man is able to love both—to love light in itself, and darkness toward the light . . . in the manifold variety of the children the variety of creation is placed before him.[4]

The fully positive meaning of this anti-hierarchical approach to teaching is unfolded at the end of "Education," again in the language of creation. "The indefinable, only factual, direction of the responsible modern educator" is toward the image of the imageless God, who is known in creation and who is answered in deeds.

When all "directions" fail there arises in the darkness over the abyss the one true direction of man towards the creative Spirit, towards the Spirit of God brooding on the face of the waters, towards Him of whom we know not whence He comes and whither He goes.

That is man's true autonomy which no longer betrays, but responds.

Man, the creature, who forms and transforms the creation, cannot create. But he, each man, can expose himself and others to the creative Spirit. And he can call upon the Creator to save and perfect His image.[5]

Distance and Relation

In seeking for the ontological basis of the alternation between I-Thou and I-It, Buber has formulated two essential movements of distancing and relation which express in philosophical form the basic paradox of biblical creation. This paradox, as we have seen, is that God sets the world and man at a distance and yet remains in relationship with them, and that He gives man ground on which to stand and yet that the very meaning of man's free standing on this ground is that he can go forth to meet the Creator who addresses him in every aspect of his creation. In Buber's philosophical anthropology "the primal setting at a distance" is the ontological presupposition for the second movement; for we can only enter into relation with being that has been set at a distance from us and thereby has become an independent opposite. Only through this act of setting at a distance does man have a "world," and only through it can he enter into relation, as an individual self, with those like himself. Distance is given to man as man, yet it is, ontologically speaking, pre-personal; that is, it precedes the I-Thou and I-It relations which make up personal existence. This distance given, man is able to enter into relation with other beings over against him; for the "overcoming" of distance does not mean simple unity but the polar tension of distance and relation together. Entering into relation is an act of the whole being—it is *the* act by which we constitute ourselves as human, and it is an act which must be repeated ever again in ever new situations. But it also belongs to our created freedom that we can enlarge, develop, accentuate, and shape the distance itself, thus changing the whole situation by making the other being into one's object. This thickening of the distance is the I-It relation, which is an elaboration of the given as the I-Thou relationship is not.

Revelation and the Thou

For Buber, as for Rosenzweig, revelation does not leave the circle of I and Thou. It is inseparable from the biblical understanding of the word as a dynamic event *between* God and man. Knowledge, from this point of view, means mutual contact and communication rather than a detached observation of an object. The reality of the sense-world is founded upon the meeting of man and God—hearing and responding to the address of all creation. The signs of address constantly happen between man and the world, not objective signs that are there to be interpreted, nor subjective projections of human significance, but the address that comes to you from the unique present when you become aware that *you* are the person addressed. What we can know of God when we are addressed by these signs of life is never accessible apart from that address. Yet from a succession of such "moment Gods" there may arise for us with a single identity "the Lord of the Voice." Each new Thou renews in all presentness the past experiences of Thou, so that the moments of the past and the moment of the present become simultaneously present and joined in living unity.

I-Thou Knowing and I-It Knowledge

This is not just an approach to religious revelation but to the theory of knowledge in general. The I-Thou relationship is a direct knowing that gives one neither knowledge about the Thou over against one nor about oneself as an objective entity apart from this relationship. It is "the genuinely reciprocal meeting in the fulness of life between one active existence and another." Although this dialogical knowing is direct, it is not entirely unmediated. The directness of the relationship is established not only through the mediation of the senses but also of the "word." The "word" may be identified with subject-object, or I-It, knowledge while it remains indirect and symbolic, but it is itself the channel and expression of I-Thou knowing when it is taken up into real dialogue. Even our knowing of the nonhuman world is, in the first instance, dialogue. What Psalm 19 says of nature—"Day unto day utters speech and night unto night voice"—Buber expresses more abstractly in his I-Thou relationship with nature. "There is no speech, neither is their voice heard," yet the things of this world do address us and come to meet us. "In the presentness of meeting," I explain in *Martin Buber: The Life of Dialogue,*

> are included all those things which we see in their uniqueness and for their own selves, and not as already filtered through our mental categories for purposes of knowledge or use. In this presentness it is no longer true . . . that the existing beings over against us cannot in some sense move to meet us as we them . . . We can feel the impact of their active reality even though we cannot know them as they are in themselves or describe that impact apart from our relation to it.[6]

Buber's attitude toward biblical revelation parallels that of his philosophy of religion in general. Some schools of Bible criticism tend to stress the literal truth of the Bible or an utter transcendence of the Word of God that reduces man's part to mere acceptance. Others have substituted "inspiration" for revelation and have reduced the Bible to "Living Literature"—a merely immanent, subjective affair expressive of man's highest spiritual strivings but not witnessing to any concrete meeting with God in history. In contrast to these two approaches, Buber sees the Bible as the record of the real meetings in the course of history between a group of people and the divine. The Bible is not primarily devotional literature, nor is it a symbolic theology which tells us of the nature of God as he is in himself. It is "anthropogeny," the historical account of God's relation to man seen through man's eyes.

> Again and again God addresses man and is addressed by him. . . . The basic teaching which fills the Hebrew Bible is that our life is a dialogue between the above and below. . . . The Bible has, in the form of a glorified remembrance, given

vivid, decisive expression to an ever-recurrent happening. In the infinite language of events and situations, eternally changing, but plain to the truly attentive, transcendence speaks to our hearts at the essential moments of personal life. And there is a language in which we can answer it; it is the language of our actions and attitudes, our reactions and our abstentions; . . . This fundamental interpretation of our existence we owe to the Hebrew Bible.[7]

Revelation, to Buber, is man's meeting with God's presence rather than information about his essence. As a result, Buber cannot believe that "finished statements about God were handed down from heaven to earth." Rather, human substance is melted by divine fire in such a way that the word that results, while human in its meaning and form, still "witnesses to Him who stimulated it and to His will." The biblical text reveals man's meeting with the divine, however, only when the reader opens himself to the text and enters into real dialogue with it.

The man of today has no access to a sure and solid faith, nor can it be made accessible to him. . . . But if he is really serious, he too can open up to this book and let its rays strike him where they will. . . . But to this end, he must read the Jewish Bible as though it were something entirely unfamiliar, as though it had not been set before him ready-made, at school and after in the light of "religious" and "scientific" certainties; as though he has not been confronted all his life with sham concepts and sham statements which cited the Bible as their authority. . . . He must yield to it, withhold nothing of his being, and let whatever will occur between himself and it. He does not know which of its sayings and images will overwhelm him and mold him, from where the spirit will ferment and enter into him, to incorporate itself anew in his body. But he holds himself open. . . . The contemporary character of this man becomes itself a receiving vessel.[8]

Revelation is never past, it is always present. Revelation is not written text but speaking Voice, speaking in the present moment and for the present situation in all its concreteness. "A generation can only receive the teachings in the sense that it renews them." What is given to an individual in this present moment leads to the understanding of the great revelations, but the vital fact is one's own personal receiving and not what was received in former times. "At all times," writes Buber, "only those persons really grasped the Decalogue who literally felt it as having been addressed to themselvles." Although the forms of religious tradition help to keep that tradition living, they are not this living tradition itself and may even choke off its flow when they are treated as if they possessed a magical objective reality in themselves. As Abraham Heschel writes, "To be a spiritual heir, one must be a pioneer."

Turning and Redemption

The completion of creation, the response to revelation, is the beginning of redemption. Redemption, to Buber, takes place always and never. It means the bringing of ever-new layers of the world of It into the immediacy of the Thou.

Our turning from evil and taking the direction toward God is the beginning of our own redemption and that of the world. God "wishes to redeem us—but only by our own acceptance of His redemption with the turning of the whole being." Our turning is only the beginning, however, for our action must be answered by God's grace for redemption to be complete. When we go forth to meet God, he comes to meet us, and this meeting is our salvation. "It is not as though any definite act of man could draw grace down from heaven; yet grace answers deed in unpredictable ways, grace unattainable, yet not self-withholding.'' It is sense-less, therefore, to try to divide redemption into a part that is dependent on man and a part that is dependent on God. We must be concerned with our action alone before we bring it about, with God's grace alone after the action is successfully done. Neither is a part-cause. Our action is enclosed in God's action, but it is still real action. Man's action and God's grace are subsumed under the greater reality of the meeting between God and man.

The decisive turning is not merely an attitude of the soul but something effective in the whole corporeality of life. It is not to be identified with repentance, for repentance is something psychological and purely inward which shows itself outwardly only in its "consequences" and "effects." The turning "is something which happens in the immediacy of the reality between man and God." It "is as little a 'psychic' event as is a man's birth or death." Repentance is at best only an incentive to this turning, and it may even stand in the way of it if we torture ourselves with the idea that our acts of penance are not sufficient and thereby withhold our best energies from the work of the turning.

The *teshuvah,* or turning to God, is born in the depths of the soul out of "the despair which shatters the prison of our latent energies" and out of the suffering which purifies the soul. In our darkest hours we feel the hand of God reaching down to us. If we have "the incredible courage" to take the hand and let it draw us up out of the darkness, we taste the essence of redemption—the knowleldge that our "redeemer lives" (Job 19:18) and wishes to redeem us. But we must accept this redemption with the turning of our whole being; for only thus can we extricate ourselves from the maze of selfishness where we have always set our-selves as our goal and find a way to God and to the fulfill-ment of the particular task for which we are intended.

The very qualities which make us what we are constitute our special approach to God and our potential use for him. Each person is created for the fulfillment of a unique purpose. Our foremost task, therefore, is the actualizing of our unique, unprecedented, and never-recurring potentialities, and not the repetition of something that another, even the greatest, has already achieved. The way by which we can reach God is revealed to us only through the knowledge of our essential qualities and inclinations. We discover this essential quality through perceiving our "central wish," the strongest feeling which stirs our inmost being. If we lend our will to the direction of our passions, we begin the movement of hallowing which God completes. In this hallowing "the total man is accepted, confirmed, and fulfilled. This is the true integration of man."

The belief in the redemption of evil does not mean any security of salvation. The prophets of Israel "always aimed to shatter all security and to proclaim in the opened abyss of the final insecurity the unwished-for God who demands that His human creatures become real . . . and confounds all who imagine that they can take refuge in the certainty that the temple of God is in their midst." There is no other path for the responsible modern man than this "holy insecurity." In an age of the "eclipse of God," the truly religious person sets forth across the God-deprived reality to a new meeting with the nameless Meeter and on his way destroys the images that no longer do justice to God. "Holy insecurity" is life lived in the Face of God. Through genuine dialogical existence the real person takes part in the unfinished process of creation. "It is only by way of true intercourse with things and beings that man achieves true life, but also it is by this way only that he can take an active part in the redemption of the world." Redemption does not take place within the individual soul but in the world through the real meeting of God and man. Everything is waiting to be hallowed by us; for there is nothing so crass or base that it cannot become material for sanctification.

Sacramental Existence

It is because God dwells in the world that the world can be turned into a sacrament. But this does not mean that the world is objectively already a sacrament. It is only capable of becoming one through the redeeming contact with the individual. The foremost meaning of a sacrament is "that the divine and the human join themselves to each other, without merging themselves in each other, a lived beyond-transcendence-and-immanence." This covenant also takes place when two human beings consecrate themselves to each other in marriage or in brotherhood; "for the consecration does not come by the power of the human partners, but by the power of the eternal wings that overshadow both." Sacramental existence, like dialogical existence in general, involves a meeting with the other in which the eternal Thou manifests itself. The sacrament "is stripped of its essential character when it no longer includes an elemental, life-claiming and life-determining experience of the other person, of the otherness, as of something coming to meet and acting hitherwards."

Our work is enclosed in God's in such a way that each moment of redemption is perfect in itself as well as taking place in the time series of the world. These are not moments of "a mystical, timeless now." Each moment is filled with all time, for in it true presentness and the movement of history are united. This union of history and the moment involves a tension and a contradiction; for although redemption takes place at every moment, there is no definite moment in the present or the future in which the redemption of the world could be pronounced as having taken place once for all. "God's redeeming power is at work everywhere and at all times, but . . . a state of redemption exists nowhere and never."

Messianism and Trust

The core of the Messianic hope does not belong to eschatology and the margin of history where it vanishes into the timeless but to "the centre, the ever-changing centre . . . to the experienced hour and its possibility." The Messiah, the righteous one, must rise out of the historic loam of man, out of the dramatic mystery of the One facing the other. Redemption is not dependent upon Messianic calculations or any apocalyptic event, but on the unpremeditated turning of our whole world-life to God. This turning is open to the whole of mankind and to all ages, for all are face to face with redemption and all action for God's sake is Messianic action. As every sinner can find forgiveness, so every civilization can be hallowed, writes Buber, and this hallowing can take place without primitivizing or curtailment.

The Jewish belief in redemption is not, first of all, *pistis,* faith in the proposition that redemption will come at some future date, but *emuna,* trust in God whose oneness also implies the ultimate oneness of God and the world. This trust in the ultimate oneness of God and the world is a faith in the power of the spirit to penetrate and transform all impulses and desires, to uplift and sanctify everything material. It is the faith "that there is really only One Power which, while at times it may permit the sham powers of the world to accomplish something in opposition to it, never permits such accomplishment to stand." But this trust in God does not imply any illusions about the present state of the world. "The unredeemed soul refuses to give up the evidence of the unredeemed world from which it suffers, to exchange it for the soul's own salvation." The Jew experiences the world's lack of redemption perhaps more intensely than any other group, writes Buber. He feels it against his skin, tastes it on his tongue.

> He always discovers only that myserious intimacy of light out of darkness which is at work everywhere and at all times; no redemption which is different in kind, none which by its nature would be unique, which would be conclusive for future ages, and which had but to be consummated.[9]

Judaism does not neglect spiritual inwardness, as Simone Weil believed, but neither is it content with it. It demands that inward truth become real life if it is to remain truth: "A drop of Messianic consummation must be mingled with every hour; otherwise the hour is godless, despite all piety and devoutness." The corollary of this demand for the redemption of the world and not just of the individual soul is the refusal to accept the Gnostic rejection of creation—the division between the kingdom of this world and the kingdom of God which leaves the evil of the world forever unredeemable. "The world is reality, and it is reality created not to be overcome but to be hallowed." Judaism cannot accept a redemption in which half the world will be eternally damned or cut off from God: "There can be no eternity in which *everything* will not be accepted into God's atonement."

> What saved Judaism is not, as the Marcionites imagine, the fact that it failed to experience "the tragedy," the contradiction in the world's process, deeply enough; but rather that it experienced the *contradiction as theophany*. This very world, this very contradiction, unabridged, unmitigated, unsmoothed, unsimplified, unreduced, this world shall be—not overcome—but consummated. . . . It is a redemption not from the evil, but of the evil, as the power which God created for his service and for the performance of his work.[10]

Yihud, or unification, does not take place through creedal profession or magic manipulation, but through the concrete meeting of I and Thou by which the profane is sanctified and the mundane hallowed. It is "the continually renewed confirmation of the unity of the Divine in the manifold nature of His manifestations." This confirmation must be understood in a quite practical way: It is brought about through our remaining true "in the face of the monstrous contradictions of life, and especially in the face of . . . the duality of good and evil." The unification which thus takes place "is brought about not to spite these contradictions, but in a spirit of love and reconciliation."

People and Community

The "national universalism" of the prophets, writes Buber, looks to each people to contribute to redemption in its own particular way. The full response to God's address to mankind must be made not only as individuals but as peoples, and not as peoples taken as ends in themselves but as "holy peoples" working toward redemption through establishing the kingship of God. To become a "holy people" means, for Israel and for all peoples, to realize God's attribute of justice in the indirect relations of the people with one another and his attribute of love in their direct relations. It means the fulfillment of God's truth and justice on earth. "To drive the plowshare of the normative principle into the hard sod of political fact" is "a tremendously difficult undertaking, but the right to lift a historical moment into the light of super-history can be bought no cheaper."

This fulfillment can only take place if the synthesis of people, land, and work results in the coming to be of a true community; for only in true community can justice and love be realized and the people hallowed. "All holiness means union between being and thing, between being and being; the highest rung of world-holiness, however, is the unity of the human community in the sight of God.'' Only a true community can demonstrate the Absolute and point the way to the kingdom of God: ''Though something of righteousness may become evident in the life of the individual, righteousness itself can only become wholly visible in the structure of the life of a people.'' The righteousness of a people, in turn, must be based upon real communities, composed of real families, real neighborhoods, and real settlements, and upon ''the relationships of a fruitful and creative peace with its neighbours.'' The peacemaker ''is God's fellow-worker,'' but we make peace not by conciliatory words and humane projects but through making peace ''wherever we are destined and summoned to do so: in the active life of our own community and in that aspect of it which can actively help determine its relationship to another community.''

The decisive test of brotherhood is not within community but at the boundary between community and community, people and people, church and church; for this is the place where diversity of kind and mind is felt most strongly. ''Every time we stand this test a new step is taken toward a true humanity, gathered in the name of God.''[11]

Buber's Challenge to Jewish Philosophy

For Julius Guttmann, as Zwi Werblowsky points out, '' 'Jewish philosophy consists of the process in which Jewish philosophers throughout the generations take the fact of Jewish religion as they find it, and then 'elucidate and justify it.' '' This is certainly true of Buber's Jewish philosophy, as is Guttmann's claim that Jewish philosophy is never a purely and immanently Jewish creation but one that draws on alien influences, yet stamps what is received from outside with its individual and specifically Jewish character.[12] Buber's special challenge to Jewish philosophy consists in the fact that he finds in Judaism not only the content of his philosophy but his approach as well. Biblical Judaism informs not just his philosophy of Judaism but also the ontology, the epistemology, and the ethics of his general philosophy. It is this that gives the interrelated categories of creation, revelation, and redemption so central a place in his thought.

3

Revelation and Reason

Martin Buber found it necessary to distinguish between reason in its detached, autocratic form and reason as one of the bearers of that "great experience of faith that blew like a storm through all the chambers" of his being. In the latter case, if the thought remains true to its task, it may not be a system that emerges from the experience, but a connected body of thought more resolved in itself and more easily transmitted. In communicating such experiences, reason can function as a trustworthy elaborator even where no precise definitions or explanations are possible, still less logical proofs.

Elaboration is of necessity a philosophical—and that means a logicizing—task. What is important, however, is that the indispensable capacity for thought not misjudge its office and act as if it were the authoritative recipient. It is incumbent upon it to logicize the superlogical, for which the law of contradiction does not hold valid; it is incumbent upon it to hold aloof from the inner contradiction; but it may not sacrifice to consistency anything of that reality itself which the experience that has happened commands it to point to.[1]

This problem of consistency and paradox does not apply to the relationship to the "eternal Thou" alone. Every I-Thou relationship, in its combination of apartness and togetherness, already transcends our ordinary logic of same and other, A and not-A. One cannot understand real communication between person and person as based upon sameness: for then there would be nothing to communicate but only identity. Neither can it be based upon total otherness; for then there would be no possibility of communicating. Neither would a part-whole scheme help us understand this most basic of human phenomena. One must start, rather, with the anthropological fact of distancing and relating as already given. Only from there can we understand how it is possible to experience the relationship from the side of the other as well as our own by means other than simply projecting, identifying, or empathizing.

Reason and the I-Thou

Buber's approach to the place of reason in the I-Thou relationship was a product not only of his own experience and insight but of his strictly anthropological approach to philosophy:

> Since I am not authorized to philosophize by any metaphysical essences, neither of "ideas" nor of "substance" nor even of the "world reason," but must as a thinker concern myself alone with man and his relations to everything, so reason as an object of my thought is important for me only insofar as it dwells in man as a property or function.[2]

When reason is active in full cooperation with a person's other properties and functions, it can have a significant, even a leading, share in the intercourse of this person with others. But if it demands that all other faculties subordinate themselves to it, it becomes presumptuous and dubious. For an example of both, Buber cited the legitimate "corrective" office of reason in setting right an "error" in one's sense perception, more precisely its incongruity with what is common to one's fellow men. But reason "cannot replace the smallest perception of something particular and unique with its gigantic structure of general concepts, cannot by means of it contend in the grasping of what here and now confronts me."[3] For Buber, nonetheless, "irrational man" would be as partial and as much a manifestation of the I of I-It as "rational man."

"If to believe in God means to speak of him in the third person," said Martin Buber, "I do not believe in him. If it means to say Thou to him, I do." There was a sense in which Buber could affirm a continuing relationship with the eternal Thou. "In the relationship to God of the man who genuinely believes, the latent Thou is unmistakable," wrote Buber. "Even when he is not able to turn to God with collected soul, God's presence, the presence of his eternal Thou, is primally real."[4] But this primal reality of the presence was in no sense equivalent to an argument for the reality of God. Buber not only declared that he knew of no cogent proof of God's existence but also that he would reject it if it existed. There would then no longer be any difference between belief and unbelief; for "the risk of faith would no longer exist."

I have no metaphysics on which to establish my faith. . . . When I say that something has for me an ontological significance, I mean thereby to state that it is not a purely psychological event, although it encompasses such an event, or rather phenomenalizes itself "inwardly" into such a one.[5]

If Buber was not a metaphysician, neither was he a theologian. If he posited no metaphysical thesis, neither did he posit a theological one. Unlike Barth, Brunner, Niebuhr, and even Tillich, he did not begin with certain theological assumptions about the nature and attributes of God, about salvation, and about the contents of faith. By "theology" Buber meant the word *about* God, "God-talk," as the contemporary theologian puts it. Theology means a teaching about God, even if it is only a "negative one" which manifests itself as a teaching of the word of God, the Logos.

> But I am absolutely not capable nor even disposed to teach this or that about God. Certainly when I seek to explain the fact of man, I cannot leave out of consideration that he, man, lives over against God. But I cannot include God himself at any point in my explanation, any more than I could detach from history the, to me indubitable, working of God in it, and make of it an object of my contemplation. As I know no theological world history, so I know no theologial anthropology in this sense; I know only a philosophical one.[6]

The "eternal Thou" did not mean "God" for Buber. "God" meant the "eternal Thou." The "eternal Thou" was not just another, up-to-date way of reintroducing the God of the philosophers, the metaphysicians, and the theologians—the God whose existence could be proved and whose nature and attributes could be described as he is in himself apart from our relation to him.

It was the reality of the "between," of the meeting itself, and there and nowhere else did Buber find the unconditional which no fathoming of the self or soaring into metaphysical heights could reveal.

> It is not the case that God could be inferred from anything else, say from nature as its originator, or from history as its ruler, or from the subject as the self that thinks itself in it. It is not

so that something else is "given" and only then is this deduced from it. Rather, this is the being that is directly, originally, and lastingly over against us, that can legitimately only be spoken to and not spoken about.[7]

To use the language of the Postscript to *I and Thou* that Buber wrote in 1958, God is the Absolute Person who *is* not a person but *becomes* one, so to speak, to love and be loved, to know and be known by us. This is the paradox of the God of the Hebrew Bible who remains imageless and unlimited and yet enters into direct relation with us. This paradox of "a becoming of the God that is" sets Buber in contrast to the traditional metaphysics which demands the choice between an absolute that is not in relation to the world and a God who is in relation and therefore less than absolute.

Revelation and the "Between"

The paradox of biblical creation is that God gives man ground on which to stand, and yet the very meaning of man's free standing on this ground is that he can go forth to meet the Creator who addresses him in every aspect of his creation. In *The Knowledge of Man,* where Buber sought for the ontological basis of the alternation between I-Thou and I-It, he expressed this paradox in philosophical-anthropological terms, as we have seen, as the two essential movements of distancing and relating through which man becomes man. The paradox of creation carried over for Buber into that of revelation; for revelation, to Buber, was neither fixed objective truth nor free subjective inspiration, but address and response, hearing and responding to the voice that speaks to man out of creation and history. Revelation, to Buber, is inseparable from the biblical understanding of the word as a dynamic event *between* God and man. Knowledge, from this point of view, means mutual contact and communication rather than a detached observation of an object. Thus the knowing within the ordinary I-Thou relationshp and the knowing of revelation are not different in nature, however different they may be in intensity or historical impact. The "signs of address" constantly happen between man and the world, Buber wrote in "Dialogue"—not objective signs that are there to be interpreted, nor subjective projections of human significance, but the address that comes to you from the unique present when you become aware that *you* are the person addressed. What we can know of God when we are addressed by these signs of life is never accessible apart from that address; yet we are not thereby abandoned to a succession of unconnected moments without historical development or meaning.

Buber took speech back to its original primal meaning of the event happening *between,* of address and response, whether with sound or without. A radio announcement blaring into an empty room is anything you like, but it is not speech. A twisted cypress on Point Lobos speaks itself in unmistakable language to anyone who is really present to see it. The question still remains: How can Buber avoid the charge of subjectivity when he characterizes the notion of revelation as objective fact or objective truth as a false fixing down?

Ronald Hepburn's Critique of the I-Thou

Many philosophers and theologians have misunderstood Buber when they suggest that he allows no room for error in the I-Thou knowing, which would mean, as Ronald Hepburn assumes, that he asserts a pure I-Thou relationship unmixed and unmixable with I-It. In his two chapters devoted to encounter in *Christianity and Paradox,* Hepburn argues on the assumption that God is not an object to Buber but a *person,* thus focusing on the nature of what one relates to rather than the nature of the relationship. This shows no understanding of Buber's "Absolute Person" who *is* not a person but becomes one, so to speak, in man's personal meeting with him. God's "person" for Buber is not an attribute of his nature—hence a limitation—but his *act.* The only direct knowledge that Hepburn recognizes is Bertrand Russell's "knowledge by acquaintance." Hence he imagines that sense-contact and the whole world of the particular is always, in the first instance, I-It, and not, as Buber would see it, I-Thou. He confuses this direct contact with "the evidence of our senses," thus giving generalizations from the particular the status of particularity and the directness and uniqueness of I-Thou a specious universality. Here is no grasp of that bond of the absolute and the particular of which Buber speaks in *Eclipse of God,* nor of anything of the way in which I-Thou and I-It alternate. Hence Hepburn imagines a scale of ever purer and ever more general I-Thou relationships leading to some mythical, totally pure I-Thou relationship with God.

In Hepburn's thinking, the "I" is presupposed as first existing independently of other selves; and only then is there any question of the "knowledge of other minds." Having no notion of Buber's "inclusion," or experiencing the other side, he posits a false logical disjunction in which I am either entirely other than the person I encounter or I become and am identical with him. He also proceeds on the false presupposition that God to Buber is some object (of a personal nature) *over against* one, rather than the Meeter met in the "between." He speaks of a "God 'behind' the world," in the uttermost contrast to Buber who sees the eternal Thou as met ever again in the finite Thou. When Hepburn asks whether "a non-contradictory account can be given of . . . the Being who is said to be over against me in the 'encounter,' " he joins Charles Hartshorne and the metaphysicians in subjecting the "Absolute Person," who can only be met in the meeting with the concrete Thou, to Aristotle's "law of contradiction."[8] He imagines, moreover, that there are tests for the "existence, presence, and activities of *persons,*" confusing entirely the individual who can be known as an object with the person who can only be known as *person* in the I-Thou relationship and in the alternation in which the It is again and again brought into the directness and presentness of the meeting with the Thou.

Moreover, Hepburn remains under the mistaken impression that Buber sees the I-Thou relationship with God as an "analogy" with the I-Thou relationship with man rather than as directly given through the relationship. "Can we," writes Hepburn, "allow experiences of encountering God to elude absolutely every checking procedure, without a grave risk of eroding away the original analogy altogether?" To this basic misunderstanding he adds the logical error of attributing to "the skeptic who decides that the analogy has broken down" the right to conclude "that the 'enocunter' is illusory." It is not surprising that toward the end he falls back on the pure psychologism of C.B. Martin, who equates the religious way of knowing with "a 'psychological' report, like 'I feel cold,' 'I see as it were a blue star' . . . judgments" which "win their immunity at the cost of saying nothing whatever about the world outside me."[9] Thus we are back to Descartes with the self-evident existence of the isolated consciousness and the problematic and derivative existence of everything else, including other persons. In the light of all this, it seems strange that even sincere sympathizers with Buber's I-Thou philosophy, such as Malcolm Diamond, take Hepburn's critique of Buber seriously.

Revelation and the Life of Dialogue

In an early fragment Buber integrated reason into his understanding of revelation as the mutual knowing of the "between."

> Revelation is continual, and everything is fit to become a sign of revelation. What is disclosed to us in the revelation is not God's essence as it is independent of our existence, but his relationship to us and our relationship to him. We can only receive revelation when and so long as we are a whole. . . . If reason has fit itself in as one of the elements in wholeness of our substance, then it cannot happen that what is experienced in revelation contradicts it although it may contradict its earlier insights. . . . Revelation thereby summons reason to take part in its reception but also to allow itself to be stirred and renewed by it.[10]

Buber rejected with equal force a reason that could be set in opposition to faith and a faith that could be set in opposition to reason, and on the same grounds: both are bastions of the world of It, both are flights from the narrow ridge, from life lived in the holy insecurity of the meeting with the unique present. The great systems of philosophy are not fictitious, said Buber. They are announcements of *real* thought relationships to existing being. But they only exist through the subject-object relation, through spirit detaching itself in the attitude of contemplation, through tearing apart the wholeness of the concrete person. The "religious situation which accosts me is not foreseeable and foreknowable, hence cannot be caught in any religious world-continuity and in any religious world-view."[11]

Religion is a lived *complexio oppositorum* in which every religious statement is a risk pointing to the situation in which God only shows himself in the events of human existence. The life of faith is no book of rules, wrote Buber in "Dialogue." It begins when the dictionary is put down. Some of Buber's critics have assumed that this means that he conceives of dialogue without any content. This "dialogue without content" criticism is by no means uncommon, quite the reverse—so much so, indeed, that in my Introduction to *A Believing Humanism: Gleanings,* I wrote:

> Some of Buber's critics have stated that his faith is pure relationship without content—a misunderstanding which is only possible for those who have never grasped Buber's existentialism of dialogue as "grounded on the certainty that meaning of existence is open and accessible in the actual lived concrete." This is not, of course, the content of absolute objective principles, whether in the form of a theological creed or of Platonic truths . . . It is rather the wholly particular content of each moment of lived dialogue in which the reality one meets is neither subjectivized nor objectivized but *responded* to.[12]

In his "Replies to My Critics" in *The Philosophy of Martin Buber,* Buber himself wrote:

> It is for me of the highest importance that the dialogue have a conent. Only this content is so much the more important, the more concrete, the more concretizing it is, the more it does justice to the unique, the coming to be, the formed, and is also able to incorporate in it the most spiritual, not metaphorically but in reality, because the spirit seeks the body and lets speech help find it. This great concreteness, however, does not belong to the isolated word in the dictionary, where speech not

only shows us its general side, its applicability, but to the word in its living context of genuine conversation, of genuine poetry, of genuine philosophy; there first does it disclose to us the unique.[13]

Revelation is neither objective knowledge nor subjective inspiration but happening, event—life lived in dialogue. "The religious statement is the witness of this dialogue." Because man is taken into the duty of knowing, this witness is one in which the relationship of I-Thou is still illumined yet detachment has begun: "no longer I-Thou knowing, *not yet* subject-object knowing." That means that this witness points back to the I-Thou knowing, the meeting itself, but the *word* of this witness is not the *Word* of God. It is the product and expression of meeting. Still one must guard against removing the reality of this witness into one's own soul.

In revelation something happens to man from a side that is not man, not soul, not world. Revelation does not take place in man and is not to be explained through any psychologism. He who speaks of "the God in his breast" stands on the outermost rim of being: one cannot, one may not live from there. Revelation does not gush forth from the unconscious: it is mastery over the unconscious. Revelation comes as a might from without, but not in such a way that man is a vessel that is filled or a mere mouthpiece. Rather the revelation seizes the human elements that are at hand and recasts them: it is the *pure shape of the meeting.*[14]

4

Religion and Ethics

The Source of Buber's Ethics

Whether one is concerned with general questions of the relation of the "is" and the "ought" or particular questions such as "How do I know what I ought to do in this particular situation," the fundamental question of moral philosophy is the basis of moral value. The basis of Martin Buber's ethics, all, including Buber, would agree, is religion—whether this be understood as his philosophy of religion, his interpretation of the biblical Covenant, his re-creation of Hasidism, or the "Single One's" unique relation with the "Eternal Thou." In "Religion and Ethics" Buber himself gives this view the strongest support: "Always it is the religious which bestows, the ethical which receives." Yet one who tries to analyze the implications of Buber's "I-Thou" philosophy for contemporary ethical theory and concrete ethical action[1] is struck by the fact that Buber's philosophical anthropology is as important for his ethics as his philosophy of religion. What is more, the question must even arise whether the philosophy of dialogue, the I-Thou relation between person and person, cannot stand by itself as an autonomous ethic, grounded in Buber's anthropology but not necessarily tied with the relation between man and God. Could not a case be made for an independent nonreligious ethic that need only be lifted out of the larger context to take on contour and come into its own?

In Buber's philosophy and interpretation of religion, the source of the "ought" is the command and will of God; in his philosophical anthropology, the "ought" is grounded in a conception of "authentic existence." This seeming divergence appears reconcilable through the fact that Buber's philosophy of religion, like his anthropology, is centrally concerned with authentic existence while his philosophical anthropology, like his philosophy of religion, is essentially concerned with hearing and responding to what is over against one. Yet "authentic existence" in Buber's religion is found through the individual's and the people's relation with God, whereas in Buber's anthropology it is found in the relation between person and person. In the one case it is God, in the other man, who is over against man. Now, of course, we shall appeal to *I and Thou* to show that man meets the "eternal Thou" in meeting the human Thou, and to *Good and Evil* to show that the decision for the good which one makes in meeting man is equally the decision for God, that one's unique personal direction realized in one's relation to the world is one's direction to God. Yet this does not change the essential fact that Buber's philosophical anthroplogy and the ethic based on it seem to subsist without the need for "revelation" in the special religious sense of the term, while his understanding of religion and of the ethic that grows out of religion cannot.

Buber's Definition of Ethics

If then we take the question of an "autonomous" ethic as our starting point, we must explore more deeply the relation between Buber's anthropology and his philosophy of religion. Martin Buber defines the ethical as the affirmation or denial of the conduct and actions possible to one "not according to their use or harmfulness for individuals and society, but according to their intrinsic value and disvalue."

> We find the ethical in its purity only there where the human person confronts himself with his own potentiality and distinguishes and decides in this confrontation without asking anything other than what is right and what is wrong in this his own situation.

He goes on to explain that the criterion by which the distinction and decision are made may be a traditional one or one perceived by the individual himself. What really matters "is that the critical flame shoot up ever again out of the depths" and the truest source for this critical flame is "the individual's awareness of what he 'really' is, of what in his unique and nonrepeatable created existence he is intended to be."[2]

One foundation of this definition of ethics is Buber's philosophy of dialogue with its emphasis on wholeness, decision, presentness, and uniqueness. Another is his philosophical anthropology with its emphasis on the potentiality which only man has and on the direction which each man must take to become what only he can become. In both Buber's philosophy of dialogue and his philosophical anthropology, value is bound up with the question of authentic existence. Valuing to Buber must always remain attached to the full concrete situation of the human being.

Responsibility must mean responding to the address of the "lived concrete." It cannot simply float above. This means that the understanding of *authentic* human existence must grow directly out of the understanding of human existence itself. The *description* of human existence—the twofold relationship of I-Thou and I-It—is only the base and the first aspect of what, considered more fully, includes the *normative*—the question of what is authentic in human existence. To Buber one becomes a self, a person, in entering into the relation with the Thou. The problem of authentic existence arises in the difference between becoming *something* of what you can be and becoming more fully what you can be. This is the difference between a "self" for practical purposes, that is, someone who is able to hold the fragments together enough to get by and get business done, and a self in the fuller sense of a person who again and again brings the conflicting parts of himself into an active unity. It is the difference between a person who has partial, fragmentary relations with others and a person who is able ever more fully to enter into relations with others, the difference between a person who only very partially realizes his uniqueness and one who more fully realizes his unique potentialities. One cannot be human at all except in the I-Thou relation.

But it is quite possible to be human without being fully human, to fall short of realizing what we might, of authenticating one's own humanity, and that is where the normative grows imperceptibly out of the descriptive. Valuing is the growing point of human existence because we live in the present pointed toward the future, aware of possibilities, having to make decisions between "better" and "worse," having to create our own future through our response to the day-by-day address of existence. So the ontological—the "is" of human existence—must include the dimension of authentic human existence as well.

Buber's Philosophical Anthropology

Man sets man at a distance and makes him independent, writes Buber in the basic statement of his anthropology. He is therefore able to enter into relation, in his own individual status, with those like himself.

> The basis of man's life with man is twofold, and it is one—the wish of every man to be confirmed as what he is, even as what he can become, by men; and the innate capacity in man to confirm his fellowmen in this way. That this capacity lies so immeasurably fallow constitutes the real weakness and questionableness of the human race: actual humanity exists only where this capacity unfolds.

This mutual confirmation of men is most fully realized in what Buber calls "making present," an event which happens partially wherever men come together but in its essential structure only rarely. Making the other present means to imagine, quite concretely, what another man is wishing, feeling, perceiving, and thinking. It is through this making present that we grasp another as a self, that is, as a being whose distance from me cannot be separated from my distance from him and whose particular experience I can make present. This event is not ontologically complete until he knows himself made present by me and until this knowledge induces the process of his inmost self-becoming.

> For the inmost growth of the self is not accomplished, as people like to suppose today, in man's relation to himself, but . . . in the making present of another self and in the knowledge that one is made present in his own self by the other.[3]

The fundamental fact of human existence, according to Buber's anthropology, is man with man. When two individuals "happen" to each other, then there is an essential remainder which is common to them but which reaches out beyond the special sphere of each. That remainder is the basic reality, the sphere of "the between," of "the inter-human" *(das Zwischenmenschliche)*.[4] The unfolding of this sphere Buber calls the "dialogical." The psychological, that which happens within the souls of each, is only the secret accompaniment to the dialogue. Genuine dialogue can be either spoken or silent. Its essence lies in the fact that "each of the participants really has in mind the other or others in their present and particular being and turns to them with the intention of establishing a living mutual relation between himsel and them." The essential element of genuine dialogue, therefore, is "seeing through the eyes of the other" or "experiencing the other side."

"Experiencing the other side" is the full development of "making the other present." It means "imagining the real"—a "bold swinging" into the life of "the particular real person who confronts me, whom I can attempt to make present to myself just in this way, and not otherwise, in his wholeness, unity, and uniqueness."[5] One must distinguish here, accordingly, between that awareness, essential to the life of dialogue, which enables one to turn to the other and that reflexive, or "monological," awareness which turns one in on oneself and lets the other exist only as one's own experience, only as a part of oneself.

Responsibility and Conscience

Dialogue not only means awareness of what addresses one, but responsibility. Responsibility, for Buber, means responding—hearing the unreduced claim of each particular hour in all its crudeness and disharmony and answering it out of the depths of one's being. This responsibility does not exclude a person from membership in a group or community, but it means that true membership in a community includes a *boundary* to membership so that no group or person can hinder one's perception of what is spoken or one's answer from the ground of one's being. This perception is not an "inner light" from God that presents one the answer at the same time as the question. God tenders the situation, but the response comes from the "conscience"—not the routine, surface, discredited conscience, but "the unknown conscience in the ground of being, which needs to be discovered ever anew." " 'Conscience' is human and can be mistaken."[6]

Conscience, to Buber, is the voice which calls one to fulfill the personal intention of being for which he was created. It is "the individual's awareness of what he 'really' is, of what in his unique and nonrepeatable created existence he is intended to be." This presentiment of purpose is "inherent in all men though in the most varied strengths and degress of consciousness and for the most part stifled by them." When it is not stifled, it compares what one is with what one is called to become and thereby distinguishes and decides between right and wrong. It is partly through this comparison that one comes to feel guilt.

> Each one who knows himself . . . as called to a work which he has not done, each one who has not fulfilled a task which he knows to be his own, each who did not remain faithful to his vocation which he had become certain of—each such person knows what it means to say that 'his conscience smites him.'[7]

The Ground of Ethical Decision

Ethical decision, for Buber, is thus both the current decision about the immediate situation that confronts one and, through this, the decision with one's whole being for God.

Direction is apprehended through one's inner awareness of what one is meant to be, for it is this that enables one to make a decision. This is a reciprocal process, however, for in transforming and directing one's undirected energies, one comes to recognize ever more clearly what one is meant to be. One experiences one's uniqueness as a designed or preformed one, intrusted to one for execution, yet everything that affects one participates in this execution. The person who knows direction responds with the whole of his being to each new situation with no other preparation than his presence and his readiness to respond. One discovers the mystery waiting for one not in oneself, but in the encounter with what one meets.[8] The goal of creation that we are intended to fulfill is not an unavoidable destiny, but something to which we are called and to which we are free to respond or not to respond. Our awareness of this calling is not a sense of what we may become in terms of our position in society nor is it a sense of what type of person we should develop into. Direction is neither conscious conception nor subconscious fantasy. It is the primal awareness of our personal way to God that lies at the very center of our awareness of ourself as I.

As it is only in genuine relation that we find direction, so it is only in relation that true ethical decision takes place. Only he who knows the presence of the Thou is capable of decision. True decision is not partial but is made with the whole soul. There can be no wholeness "where downtrodden appetites lurk in the corners" or where the soul's highest forces watch the action, "pressed back and powerless, but shining in the protest of the spirit."[9] If one does not become what one is meant to be, if one does not bring one's scattered passions under the transforming and unifying guidance of direction, no wholeness of the person is possible. Conversely, without attaining personal wholeness, one can neither keep to direction nor enter into full relation.

Buber's discovery of the source of the moral "ought" in dialogue must not be confused with Jean-Paul Sartre's "invention" of values. Such a self-created morality means freedom without genuine responding and responsibility, just as a "moral duty" imposed from without means "responsibility" without either freedom or genuine responding. The narrow ridge between the two is a freedom that means freedom *to* respond, and a responsibility that means both address from without and free response from within. Sartre's definition of value as the meaning of life which the individual chooses, Buber points out, destroys all meaningful notion of value:

> One can believe in and accept a meaning or value . . . if one has discovered it, not if one has invented it. It can be for me an illuminating meaning, a direction-giving value, only if it has been revealed to me in my meeting with being, not if I have freely chosen it for myself from among the existing possibilities and perhaps have in addition decided with a few fellow creatures: This shall be valid from now on.[10]

Buber's concept of the responsibility of an I to a Thou is closely similar to Kant's second formulation of the categorical imperative: Never treat one's fellow or oneself as a means only but always also as an end of value in himself. But even here there is an essential difference. Kant's sentence grows out of an "ought" based on the idea of human dignity. Buber's related concept of making the other present is based on the ontological reality of the life between man and man.[11] To Kant the respect for the dignity of others grows out of one's own dignity as a rational being bound to act according to universal laws. For Buber, the concern for the other as an end in himself grows out of one's direct relation to this other and to that higher end which he serves through the fulfillment of his created uniqueness. Thus Kant's imperative is essentially subjective (the isolated individual) and objective (universal reason), whereas Buber's is dialogical. In Kant the "ought" of reason is separated from the "is" of impulse. For Buber, in contrast, "is" and "ought" join without losing their tension in the precondition of authentic human existence—making real the life between man and man.

Buber's philosophy of dialogue radically shifts the whole ground of ethical discussion by moving from the universal to the concrete and from the past to the present—in other words, from I-It to I-Thou. Buber does not start from some external, absolutely valid ethical code which man is bound to apply as best as possible to each new situation. Instead he starts with the situation itself.

> The idea of responsibility is to be brought back from the province of specialized ethics, of an "ought" that swings free in the air, into that of lived life. Genuine responsibility exists only where there is real responding.[12]

Most of the traditional ethical values—not killing, stealing, commiting adultery, lying, cheating, and so forth—are, in fact, implied in the I-Thou relation; but not as an abstract code valid in advance of particular situations. Rather, one must move from the concrete situation to the decision as to what is the right direction in this instance. One does not go directly from a conscious precept to a moral action, for no action in which a person involved himself merely on a conscious level could really be moral in a meaningful sense of the term. What happens is that one goes from deep-seated attitudes, of which one is perhaps not fully aware, to the response to the present situation which produces the moral action. The precept and teaching may, of course, have influenced those attitudes: the person may have taken them in at some point and mixed them with himself in such a way that at some time in the future he may indeed act in a manner corresponding to the precept; but it is not by his having memorized the precept and recognized it as a universal moral injunction that this takes place. What Buber writes of the "great character" also holds true, to a lesser extent, of any responsible person's relation to moral norms.

No responsible person remains a stranger to norms. But the command inherent in a genuine norm never becomes a maxim and the fulfilment of it never a habit. Any command that a great character takes to himself in the course of his development does not act in him as a part of his consciousness or as material for building up his exercises, but remains latent in a basic layer of his substance until it reveals itself to him in a concrete way. What it has to tell him is revealed whenever a situation arises which demands of him a solution of which till then he had perhaps no idea. Even the most universal norm will at times be recognized only in a very special situation. . . . In moments like these the command addresses us really in the second person, and the Thou in it is no one else but one's own self. Maxims command only the third person, the each and the none.[13]

Where Buber's Philosophical Anthropology and Philosophy of Religion Meet

What then are we to conclude about the relation and relative importance of Buber's philosophical anthropology and his philosophy of religion as sources of his ethics? First, that Buber's ethics is directly based on and informed by his philosophical anthropology—that these two are, in fact, inseparable since the problem of what man is includes the question of authentic existence, what it means to be really human, while ethics must be grounded in a descriptive as well as normative definition of what man "is" if its "ought" is to have any meaning or force. Certainly, it is in Buber's philosophical anthropology that one can see the main categories of his ethics spelled out. Yet these very categories—awareness and response, responsibility, uniqueness, decision, direction, personal wholeness—imply, as we have seen, Buber's philosophy of religion. If man becomes authentic, if the person becomes what only he can and should become, it is through responding with his whole being to the address of the unique situation which confronts him, through becoming whole and finding his true personal direction—the direction to God. Inauthentic existence, conversely, is the failure to enter into dialogue, to attain personal wholeness, to find direction, to make true decision, to direct one's passion through making his casual relations essential ones. In what Buber calls the second stage of evil, further, a course of decisionlessness ends in an absolute affirmation of oneself and the denial of God—of any order and reality over against one that might stand in judgment of one's existence.

Buber's answer to the question of the Euthyphro, if implicit, is quite clear: God does not will in accordance with some independent order of the good; on the contrary, the very meaning of "good" and of any order of good that exists is derived from our relation to God and his demand that we make real our created existence by becoming human, becoming real. The choice for Buber is not between religion and morality, as it is for Kierkegaard, but between a religion and morality wedded to the universal and a religion and morality wedded to the concrete.

Only out of a personal relationship with the Absolute can the absoluteness of the ethical co-ordinates arise without which there is no complete awareness of self. Even when the individual calls an absolute criterion handed down by religious tradition his own, it must be reforged in the fire of the truth of his personal essential relation to the Absolute if it is to win true validity. But always it is the religious which bestows, the ethical which receives.[14]

The reason why it is always the religious which bestows and the ethical which receives is to be found in the nature of good as Buber understands it. The good, for Buber, is not an objective state of affairs or an inner feeling, but a type of relationship—the dialogue between man and man and between man and God.

Every ethos has its origin in a revelation, whether or not it is still aware of and obedient to it; and every revelation is revelation of human service to the goal of creation, in which service man authenticates himself.[15]

This means that the good cannot be referred back to any Platonic universal or impersonal order of the cosmos, nor can it be founded in any general system of utility or interest. It grows instead out of what is most particular and concrete—not the quasi-concreteness of the "empirically verifiable," but the actual present concreteness of the unique direction which one apprehends and realizes in the meeting with the everyday.

At this point, then, Buber's philosophical anthropology and his philosophy of religion converge. We are still left, however, with our original question of whether Buber's philosophy of religion implies "revelation" in a special, specifically religious sense that is not implied by his anthropology. Is the "personal relationship with the absolute" out of which the ethical receives its absoluteness and each man achieves his awareness of self the same as the "revelation" in which "every ethos has its origin," the revelation of "human service to the goal of creation . . . in which man authenticates himself''? ''The powerful revelations to which the great religions appeal are essentially the same as the quiet ones that happen at all places and all times,'' writes Buber in *I and Thou*. And this view is carried forward: ''What is given to an individual in this present moment leads to the understanding of the great revelations, but the vital fact is one's own personal receiving and not what was received in former times.''[16]

In one of his late statements on revelation, Buber distinguished between historical revelations, which are objectifiable and communicable precisely because they are historical and have entered into the life of a group in a given hour of history, and personal revelations without known historical results. These latter cannot be dealt with or communicated, for they do not exist at all ''objectively.''

> But every person open to the influx of the message conveyed by everyday events could and should know that there is no *absolute* difference between such a message and what we call by the name of revelation. What differs, essentially, is the degree of certainty.

Even this difference in certainty is not a great one for the modern man who, like Buber himself, cannot go back on his knowledge of the inmixture of human substance in the historical revelation in which the divine flame nonetheless dwells, never to be distinguished from it. But neither can such men ''renounce the historical tradition that has moulded them religiously.''

> What they can and must do, is to listen again and again, in order to learn which of the commandments of tradition can be heard by them as being commanded by God to them, and of course to live consequently. This can be done only in the stern responsibility of faith.[17]

Buber on the Kierkegaardian "Suspension of the Ethical"

We must conclude, therefore, that Buber's own working attitude toward the relation between religion and ethics is closer to the "fear and trembling" of the "Single One," as he describes him, than to the essential certainty of the Hasidic community in whose highest hours the separate spheres of religion and ethics merge into human holiness.[18] In "The Question to the Single One" Buber modifies Kierkegaard's conception by insisting that the Single One must have essential relations to the creature as well as to the Creator, that he must belong to the group while preserving a boundary line to his membership to the group. Yet he preserves the individual responsibility before God and the "fear and trembling" with which man dares his stammering answer to God's address. In his Hasidic essay, "Love of God and Love of Neighbor," Buber refers to this same position as that of a type of man "especially significant for our age . . . the man who does not have the faith that he knows with assurance through a tradition what God commands him to do in his life."

He regards the traditional revelation as a fusion of the divine and the human. . . . Certainly, he receives from all things and events a divine claim on his person, but in general no indication is thereby given to him as to what he should do for God in this hour, in this situation; rather at most, so to speak, a question is directed to him that he must fill in with his own doing and not doing. . . . There are, certainly, hours in which he acts as with full authority, but, also those in which he experiences complete abandonment, and between the two runs his life.[19]

What this means in practice is seen in Buber's incisive criticism of Kierkegaard's conception of "the suspension of the ethical.'' Buber does not deny Kierkegaard's starting point: that God's command to Abraham to sacrifice his son Isaac was a unique revelation by God that could not be put into any framework of universal morality. But Buber does deny the consequences that Kierkegaard draws from this. Kierkegaard turns the unique situation of Abraham into a more general and equivocal one in which the "knight of faith" must decide for himself who is the "Isaac" whom God wants him to sacrifice. More important still, Kierkegaard takes for granted what even the Bible could not: that the Voice one hears is always the voice of God, that the only right response is obedience.

> Abraham, to be sure, could not confuse with another the voice which once bade him leave his homeland. . . . It can happen, however, that a sinful man is uncertain whether he does not have to sacrifice his (perhaps also very beloved) son to God for his sins (Micah 6:7). For Moloch imitates the voice of God. In contrast to this, God Himself demands of this as of every man (not of Abraham, His chosen one, but of you and me) nothing more than justice and love, and that he 'walk humbly' with Him, with God (Micah 6:8)—in other words, not much more than the fundamental ethical.[20]

Ours is an age, says Buber, in which the Kierkegaardian suspension of the ethical for the sake of the religious fills the world in a caricaturized form. Everywhere, over the whole surface of the human world, false absolutes pierce unhindered through the level of the ethical and demand "the sacrifice" of personal integrity in order that equality may come, that freedom may come, or that the Kingdom may come. "In the realm of Moloch honest men lie and compassionate men torture. And they really and truly believe that brother-murder will prepare the way for brotherhood!"

The cure for this situation is not returning to some ob-

jective, universal order of ethics, but the rise of a new conscience which will summon men to guard with the innermost power of their souls against the confusion of the relative with the Absolute. The limits, the limitedness of the
false Absolute must be discovered by that "incorruptible
probing glance"[21] which comes to those who stand their
ground in each situation anew and meet it in all its uniqueness. If the "fundamental ethical" thus remains a part of
the life of dialogue, this does not imply the special revelation that God makes to Abraham, "His chosen one," but
only that dialogue between man and man which is at the
same time a dialogue between man and God—a personal
revelation, but not necessarily a historical one.

It is misleading, therefore, to overemphasize the part
which revelation plays in Martin Buber's ethics unless one
keeps in mind that he is here referring primarily to the
"everyday revelation" of Micah rather than the excep-
tional historical revelation of Abraham. The life of the individual, of course, is set in history, and history cannot be
understood apart from the historical revelation in the Bible
and elsewhere. But it is not on this that Buber's moral philosophy—insofar as we may delimit such a sphere within
the totality of his thought—decisively depends.

5

Existential Guilt, Existential Trust, and the Eternal Thou

Buber on Heraclitus and the Eastern Mystics

There are two other sources which we must look at in connection with our problem of the bases of Buber's ethics—both late developments in his philosophical anthropology. The one is his essay, "What is Common to All"— a study of Heraclitus that sets Heraclitus' injunction, "One should follow the common," in contrast with Taoist, Hindu, and modern mystical teachings which Buber characterizes as a flight from "the arch reality out of which all community stems—human meeting." By denying the uniqueness of the human person, these teachings annihilate it, one's own person as well as the other; for human existence and the intercourse of men that grows out of it is the chance for meeting in which each says to the other, not "I am you," but "I accept you as you are. . . . Here first is uncurtailed existence."

That Buber's basis for this distinction between Heraclitus and the Eastern teachings is, in the first instance, his anthropology, with its conception of authentic existence, rather than his philosophy of religion as such, is made clear by his criticism of Aldous Huxley's counsel to the use of the mescalin drug:

> Man may master as he will his situation, to which his surroundings also belong; he may withstand it, he may alter it, he may, when it is necessary, exchange it for another; but the fugitive flight out of the claim of the siutaiton into situationlessness is no legitimate affair of man. And the true name of all paradises which man creates for himself by chemical or other means is situationless-ness.[1]

While man has his thoughts and experiences as "I," it is as "We" that he raises these thoughts and experiences into being itself, into just that mode of existence that Buber calls "the between." Nor is this We, in any sense, of a secondary or merely instrumental importance. It is basic to existence as such, and in an age such as ours "in which the true meaning of every work is encompassed by delusion and falsehood and the original intention of the human glance is stifled by tenacious mistrust," man is threatened with ceasing to exist at all if he does not recover the genuineness of speech and existence as We. Even the mystic who turns away form the We to a deepened contemplation of existing being is still fleeing from the "leaping fire" with which, in his seventh epistle, Plato describes the dynamics between persons in the We.

> The flight from the common cosmos into a special sphere that is understood as the true being is, in all its stages, from the elemental sayings of the ancient Eastern teachings to the arbitrariness of the modern counsel to intoxication, a flight from the existential claim on the person who must authenticate himself in We. It is a flight from the authentic spokenness of speech in whose realm a repsonse is demanded, and response is responsibility.[2]

It is particularly remarkable that Buber rests his case against the Taoist, Vedantist, and modern mystic primarily on anthropological grounds, since we are confronted here with basic differences in the understanding of reality, meaning, and value that are, in the last instance, religious in nature. No nondualist Vedantist would be troubled by Buber's criticism, since for him true "personal" existence and the true We are found precisely on the road that Buber holds annihilates them. On the other hand, the common "logos" of speech and response is not merely a similarity between Heraclitus and the biblical prophets, as Buber points out. It is grounded much more securely in the biblical view of existence as the dialogue between man and God than in Heraclitus' concept of a reality that "was and is and ever shall be ever living Fire." And Buber himself recognizes this limitation to the possibility of enregistering Heraclitus' teaching of the common in the "life of dialogue":

> What he designates as the common has nothing that is over against it as such: logos and cosmos are, to him, self-contained; there is nothing that transcends them. . . . No salvation is in sight for us, however, if we are not able again "to stand before the face of God" in all reality as a We—as it is written in that faithful speech that once from Israel . . . started on its way.[3]

Unhappily, Buber concludes with this paragraph. He does not, as we should have liked, explain to us wherein the common logos and cosmos of Heraclitus was lacking—as dialogue?—as authentic existence itself, in its historical dimension?—or in the dimension of religious revelation? However, we can, in any case, conclude that Buber is here recognizing that the ultimate (even if not the immediate) base for his view of authentic existence, and for the anthropology in which it is set, is religious. Whether this religious base implies, further, a special historical revelation generically different from the revelation that comes in the common speech-with-meaning that makes us a We—about this we cannot reach a conclusion. We can retain our original hypothesis, nontheless, if we interpret this final disclaimer to mean, first, that real existence as a We is not possible in a self-contained cosmos, but only in ever-renewed dialogue with what is over against one; and second, that although one stands in a We through actual or potential relations between person and person, the We, too, must sometimes be like an I. To find its own true existence, it too has to enter into relation with the Thou that confronts it—the Thou of other nations, of history, of God.

Existential Guilt

Buber's treatment of guilt takes us a step further still in understanding the relation between his anthropology and his philosophy of religion. "Original guilt consists in remaining with oneself," Buber says in "What is Man?" But in "Religion and Ethics," as we have seen, guilt arises from not becoming what one is called to become, not remaining faithful to a task or vocation one has become certain of. Guilt in this case is the product of not taking the direction toward God. But since the direction toward God is found in the meeting with what one encounters in each new hour, we can say at one and the same time that the guilty man is he who shuns the dialogue with God and he who does not enter into the dialogue with man and the world.

In "Guilt and Guilt Feelings," however, Buber distinguishes between three interrelated levels on which one must deal with guilt and reconciliation—the legal, the personal, and the religious. These levels can only be understood in the context of the basic distinction of the essay—that between "groundless" neurotic guilt which is a subjective feeling within a person and "existential guilt," which is an ontic, interhuman reality in which the person dwells. The standpoint from which we must apprehend existential guilt is not that of the repression of social or parental reprimands but "the real insight into the irreversibility of lived time, a fact that shows itself unmistakably in the starkest of all human perspectives, that concerning one's own death." This insight shows us the impossibility of recovering the original point of departure or repairing what has been done. Swept along in the torrent of time, the self in guilt shudders with the realization that he, who has become another, is nonetheless identical with himself, the man whose action or failure to act has burdened him with guilt. The existential discovery of time as a torrent is identical, therefore, with the existential discovery of personal responsibility as extending over time.

Existential guilt is "guilt that a person has taken on himself as a person and in a personal situation." But this personal guilt is at the same time and by the same token objective, or rather dialogical, guilt which transcends the realm of inner feelings and of the self's relation to itself: "Existential guilt occurs when someone injures an order of the human world whose foundations he knows and recognizes as those of his own existence and of all common human existence." This "order of the human world" is not an objective absolute existing apart from man: it is the interhuman itself, the genuine We, the common logos and cosmos in Buber's interpretation of Heraclitus. The objective relationship in which each man stands toward others and through which he is able to expand his environment *(Umwelt)* into a world *(Welt)* "is his share in the human order of being, the share for which he bears responsibility." This objective relationship can rise through existential participation into a personal relation; but it can also be merely tolerated, neglected, or injured, and the injury of the relationship is an injury at this place of the human order of being. Buber indicates, correspondingly, a threefold response to existential guilt:

> first, to illuminate the darkness that still weaves itself about the guilt . . . second, to persevere . . . in that newly won humble knowledge of the identity of the present person with the person of that time; and third, in his place and according to his capacity, in the given historical and biographical situations, to restore the order-of-being injured by him through the relation of an active devotion to the world.[4]

The Three Spheres of Reconciliation

Now, however, Buber distinguishes between three different, though related, spheres in which the reconciliation or reparation of guilt can take place: first, the sphere of the law of society in which confession of guilt is followed by penalty and indemnification; second, the sphere of conscience with its three stages of illumination, perseverance, and reconciliation; and "the third and highest sphere, that of faith." In this last sphere "the action commences within the relation between the guilty man and his God and remains therein," and it is likewise consummated in three events: confession of sin, repentance, and penance. The sphere of conscience is the sphere of real existential guilt which arises out of man's being "and for which he cannot take responsibility without being responsible to his relationship to his own being." Buber does not speak of guilt here, as he does in "Religion and Ethics," as the denial of the created task to which one is called. All the more significant, therefore, is the relationship which Buber indicates between the separate spheres of conscience and of faith.

This relationship is already implicit in reconciliation, as

Buber understands it: reconciliation is only valid, he writes, if it happens "out of the core of a transformed relationship to the world, a new service to the world with the renewed forces of the renewed man." Although, as we may suppose, such tranformation can take place outside the sphere of faith, it is preeminently in that sphere that man's whole existence becomes involved and renewed. Man is never guilty toward himself alone. He "is always guilty toward other beings as well, toward the world, toward the being that exists over against him." Reconciliation, accordingly, must mean reconciliation with others, with the world, and with the reality that he meets ever again, the "eternal Thou." Not as if the sphere of conscience is swallowed by the sphere of faith, but the two exist separately and together at once:

> For the sincere man of faith, the two spheres are so referred to each other in the practice of his life, and most especially when he has gone through existential guilt, that he cannot trust himself exclusively to either of them.[5]

Both spheres can err; both—conscience not less than faith—must place themselves in the hands of grace. If Buber will not speak "of the inner reality of him who refuses to believe in a transcendent being with whom he can communicate," he does report the way in which existential guilt, hence the sphere of the conscience, leads to a personal transformation in which the sphere of the conscience and that of faith are indistinguishable:

> I have met many men in the course of my life who have told me how, acting from the high conscience as men who had become guilty, they experienced themselves as seized by a higher power. These men grew into an existential state to which the name of rebirth is due.[6]

The Self Is Not Its Own Goal

Can we say, then, that it is possible to carve out of Buber's philosophy an autonomous ethics, free from a necessary connection with religion? Yes and no. Yes, if we mean by religion a separate sphere of special, specifically religious revelation and command; no, if we understand God's "Where art thou, Adam?" to be addressed to every man at every hour through each everyday event that confronts him for then "religion" is simply man's listening and responding to this address.

But it is precisely here that the problem of the bases of Buber's ethics becomes most acute. For if I find authentic existence in the meeting with the Thou over against me, I cannot make that meeting a means to the end of attaining authentic existence without reducing my partner to an It and robbing the meeting of all its genuineness, including its beneficial effect on my own existence. "What humanity is," and hence what I am, "can be grasped only in vital reciprocity." "There resides in every man the possibility of attaining authentic existence in the special way peculiar to him," writes Buber. This basic assumption of Buber's anthropology is clearly founded on his understanding of creation, and attaining authentic existence means here fulfillment of the unique task given one in one's very creation. Here, at its deepest point, therefore, Buber's anthropology clearly rests on a philosophy of religion which is itself nothing other than a pointing to an individual and historical relation to the eternal Thou, a pointing to that *emuna,* or trust in the relation with God, which is the basic reality of biblical faith. The concern for authentic personal existence, hence, can never mean that the self is its own goal.

The self as such is not ultimately the essential, but the meaning of human existence given in creation again and again fulfills itself as self. . . . The dynamic glory of the being of man is first bodily present in the relation between two men each of whom in meaning the other also means the highest to which this person is called, and serves the self-realization of this human life as one true to creation.[7]

Thus we are pointed back to the concrete, particular I-Thou relationship both for the general source of value and the specific answer to the question, "What ought I to do in this situation?"

Responsibility and Relationship

It would be a mistake to understand the "ought" that arises out of this ethic to mean that one ought every moment to be in an I-Thou relationship, as if that were an ideal to aim for. The "ought" that is asked of one is the *quantum satis*—what one is capable of at any moment. And only the person himself can know what this is and then only in the situation itself, not before.

One does not learn the measure and limit of what is attainable in a desired direction otherwise than through going in this direction. The forces of the soul allow themselves to be measured only through one's using them.[8]

Sometimes one is capable of very little indeed, sometimes more than one dreamed possible; for what one is able to do, his potentiality, is called out of him in responding to the situation. This means that the "ought" grows out of the particular interrelation of I-Thou and I-It in that situation.

In *I and Thou* Buber defines "love" not as a feeling within each partner, but as a supra-individual reality *between* the two. This betweenness, however, is the responsibility of an I *for* a Thou and not just *to* him. "Dialogue" means "our entering . . . into the situation which has at this moment stepped up to us, whose appearance we did not know and could not know, for its like has not yet been." Yet there must also be the continuity of being responsible *for* what we have responded *to*:

> A situation of which we have become aware is never finished with, but we subdue it into the substance of lived life. Only then, true to the moment, do we experience a life that is something other than a sum of moments. We respond to this moment, but at the same time we respond on its behalf, we answer for it. A newly-created concrete reality has been laid in our arms; we answer for it. A dog has looked at you, you answer for its glance, a child has clutched your hand, you answer for its touch, a host of men moves about you, you answer for their need.[9]

Our responsibility for another does not prevent our having an I-Thou relation to someone else than he. Nonetheless, it is a commitment that in some way limits our possibilities of new response, a "fidelity," as Gabriel Marcel would put it, that binds the past and the present with the future. This continued responsibility is implicit in Buber's treatment of existential guilt: the first response to it, as we have seen, must be the illuminating recognition of the fact of guilt and of the fact that I, who am so different from what I was, am nonetheless identical with the person who injured the common existence in the past and caused the guilt that I carry; the second stage is the perseverance in this self-identification; and the third the reconciliation with the injured order of being at whatever point is possible to me, including, if it can still be done, approaching the person toward whom I am guilty in the light of my self-illumination, acknowledging to his face my existential guilt, and helping him, insofar as possible, to overcome the consequences of my guilty action.[10]

The continuity of being "responsible for" a Thou as well as responsive to him is essential for an ethic of personal relations that includes continuing, committed relationships such as friendship, love, marriage, the relationship between teacher and student, therapist and patient, pastor and congregant. Spontaneity does not mean gratuitous, arbitrary action; for response with the whole being includes all that one has been, including one's past I-Thou relations with this person and others. Although it is true, moreover, that it is only in an I-Thou relationship that I apprehend the unique value of the other and am able to experience his side of the relationship and know what can help him, still I do not necessarily cease to deal lovingly with him even when he is no longer Thou for me in any but a formal sense.

Since the human Thou must constantly become an It, one is ultimately responsible to the eternal Thou who never becomes an It. But it is just in the concrete that we meet the eternal Thou, and it is this which prevents dialogue from degenerating into "repsonsibility" to an abstract moral code or universal idea. Man is created in the image of God. But I do not respect my fellowman as deduction from this premise. On the contrary, I realize him as created in the image of God only when I meet him in his concrete uniqueness as Thou. What is meant by love thy neighbor, if it is to become real and not just remain a warm glow in one's heart, can only be discovered in the situation. The I-Thou relation, similarly, is the only relationship in which I discover that men are equal in the only way that they really are equal—that each is of unique value, of value in himself, and that in the meeting with this unique other my own existence is authenticated.

In that relation which claims my whole being, which I must enter as a person, and in which I find the meaning of my existence, in that relation which calls me forth and to which I respond, in that relation of freedom, direction, mutuality, and presentness, there is no room left over to speak of a separate relationship with God. No matter how "inward" he may be, the "religious" man still lives in the world. If he does not have an I-Thou relation with the world, therefore, he necessarily makes the world into an It. He treats it solely as a means for his sustenance and an object for his contemplation. "He who knows the world as something by which he is to profit, does not know God otherwise."[11]

This does not mean, however, that there is a relation to the eternal Thou only at the moments when there is an *actual* relation to the human Thou. Then our moral responsibility might seem to be subject to the same discontinuity and fragility as our human relationships themselves. In *I and Thou* Buber speaks of the meeting with the temporal Thou as at the same time a meeting with the eternal Thou: "In each process of becoming that is present to us . . ., in each *thou* we address the eternal *Thou*, the *Thou* in which the parallel lines of relations meet." But he also speaks of the relation to the eternal Thou as summons and sending and of the primal twofold movement of "estrangement from" and "turning toward" the primal Source.

> Every real relationship in the world fulfills itself in the interchange of actuallity and latency. . . . But in the pure relationship the latency is only the holding of breath of the actuality, in which the Thou remains present. . . . In the great privilege of the pure relationship the privileges of the world of It are suspended. By virtue of it there exists the continuity of the world of Thou: the isolated moments of relationship unite into a world-life of solidarity.[12]

Does not this mean that we relate to the present and actual eternal Thou even when the temporal Thou has again become only past and potential, that is, when it has again become It? This does not mean that we have a relation to the eternal Thou apart from our relation to the temporal Thou; but that our relation to the eternal Thou is the very foundation of our relation to the temporal Thou if the latter is understood deeply enough. That we are able ever again to meet as Thou either the person who was Thou for us but is now It, or some other whom we have never before related to as Thou, already implies a continuing, even though not continuous, relation with the Thou that does not become It. It is this potentiality of his being, or again being a Thou for us, that ultimately prevents—if anything does—our treating the man whom we do not know as Thou, purely as a dispensable It. And this "potential Thou" rests not only on the "actual Thou" of remembered I-Thou relationships, but on the "Actual Thou" of Present Reality—the relation to the eternal Thou "in which potential is still actual being."

They key difference between the eternal and the temporal Thou in this respect is that within the very meaning of the former, I-It is also real—that no existent is so Godforsaken that it is cut off from reality, no existence so Godforsaken that it is by its very nature cut off from *real* existence. Even the movement away from relationship is a part of the reality of relationship itself. Trust is trust that there is meaning in the world: it is trust in the world as a world of *potential* Thou. Although again and again in particular situations the Thou and the It are opposed, this trust implies the conviction that ultimately they stand in a dialectical rather than a dualistic relation to each other, that they are, as Buber himself puts it, "two world aspects" rather than "two worlds."[13]

The Interaction of I-Thou and I-It

We can understand the problematics of this trust more fully if we turn from the general questions that arise concerning Buber's moral philosophy to the very real problems that confront us as soon as we have to make a difficult moral decision, sacrificing one person or another, one value or another, one goal or another. How do we arrive at a moral decision when we are responsible to more than one Thou and these responsibilities seem incompatible? How are we to distinguish within a particular relationship between I-Thou and I-It relations, how can we know which, in fact, dominates and when I-Thou may really be a front for I-It? How do we know when a friendship is a true one? How are we to distinguish between that element in a guilt feeling that is based on "existential guilt" and that which is "groundless" and neurotic? How do we know when we are responding with the whole being? How do we know that what we take to be a whole response is not really so intense a partial response that we are unaware of the parts that are suppressed?

These problems point us back in turn to a special problem in the interrelation and interaction of I-Thou and I-It. Since "evil" is defined by Buber as the domination of the Thou by the It and since such evil does exist and again and again vitiates human relations, we cannot take it for granted that any particular I-It relation is a potential I-Thou in the sense of a direct movement being possible from that situation to an I-Thou relation.

It is necessary to distinguish here between two stages in the transition from I-Thou to I-It. First, there is that which as social structure, convention, or agreement, or, in the case of knowledge, as word, symbol, or image, points back directly to the unique reciprocal contact and knowing of particular I-Thou relationships. Second, there is that which, because it takes the form of self-perpetuating structures or abstract and general categories, no longer leads or points back to the meeting with the concrete and the unique, but instead takes its place and blocks the return.

The first stage of I-Thou relation or knoweldge is a primary level of abstraction and objectification that derives directly form the concrete meeting with the Thou and may lead back to it again. It may also serve, however, as material for still further objectification and structuring. Once this second step is accomplished, it cannot so easily lead directly back to the particular I-Thou meeting, even though it may originally derive from it. In direct and reciprocal relationships themselves, what may once have been genuine mutual relation may become a formality or a pretense, from which position a direct return to the I-Thou may be impossible. The trust in the potential Thou, accordingly, cannot mean the trust that any particular relationship will ascend or reascend from It to Thou; but only the refusal to exclude any relationship *in principle* from that possibility.

The very limits of our existence make it necessary for every temporal Thou to become an It. Where then is the meaning, the reality that I find in the meeting with the parlticular Thou who becomes an It? Through each Thou I meet *the* Thou—I do not meet the same Thou, in the sense of an "essence of Thou" or a particular form of Thou, but once again I find present meaning, present reality. Ultimately we can find no continuity or security beyond this. If I trust in a person, a relationship, this means that despite what may and will happen, I enter relationship again and bring all the past moments of Thou and the moments of It too into present meeting. The particular person to whom I now say Thou may die, become sick, become disturbed; he may betray me, rupture the relationship, or simply turn away and fail to respond. And sooner or later something of this does happen for most of us. When it does, it is trust too which enables us to remain open and respond to the new address of the new situation.

Trust in Existence

To relate to the eternal Thou means that, despite the fact that we cannot possibly preserve a smooth continuity of relations with the temporal Thou, we find the full meaning of our existence by again and again bringing the world into our relationship with the Thou. If we lose our trust in existence, conversely, we are no longer able to enter anew into relationship. The "existential mistrust" between man and man stems from the destruction of trust in human existence itself. "At its core the conflict between mistrust and trust of man conceals the conflict between the mistrust and trust of eternity."[14]

Trust means trust in this present which I am never going to grasp fully with my mind since there are always at least two points of view, two realities which can never be included in any single perspective—my own existence and what is over against me. It also means trust in the future—trust that we may meet the Thou again in a new form and a new situation. These two trusts supplement each other. If we had no trust in the present Thou, then neither could we trust in the future one. But if we had no trust in the future, then we would lose even what we did have in the present: the mistrust of existence itself would enter as a corroding force into every relationship making impossible full acceptance of the present and going out to meet it with our whole being. Then the present would indeed become nothing but a vanishing moment in which the future is forever going over into the past. Ultimate trust—trust in existence itself—is trust in the present and future at once. It is trust in the God who will be there even as he will be there, who will be with us even when we walk, as we will, in the valley of the shadow of death. It is this God who is *re*cognized in each genuine meeting with the utterly new, the utterly unique.

It is, then, our trust in the eternal Thou, or trust in existence itself, that ultimately gives actuality and continuity to our discontinuous and often merely potential relations to the human Thou. And it is this trust, too, that gives continuity and reality to our own existence as persons; for in itself personality is neither continuous nor always actual. If it is the confirmation of others and our own self-confirmation that gets us over the gaps and breaks in the first instance, it is our trust in existence itself that enables this individual course to become a personal direction rather than a meaningless flux. Without a personal relationship with the Absolute, as Buber has said, "there is no complete awareness of self."

We meet the eternal Thou only in our existence as persons, only in our meeting with the other: we cannot know it as if from outside this existence. The philosopher who recognizes this "must renounce the attempt to include God in his system in any conceptual form." He must "point toward God, without actually dealing with him."[15] The philosophy of dialogue precludes, therefore, even the most creative and organic of process philosophies and on this account alone invalidates the attempt which some have made to subsume Buber's philosophy of religion under Whitehead's metaphysics.[16] The Thou confronts us with the unexpected, takes us unawares. We must stand our ground yet be prepared to go forth again and again to meet we know not what. It is not insight into process but trust in existence that enables us to enter into any genuine meeting with the unique reality that accosts us in the new moment.

The Link between Ethics and Philosophy of Religion

There is often a correlation between a thinker's approach to ethics and his approach to philosophy of religion. Those thinkers who feel that religion is solidly founded only when it rests on proofs of the existence of God that put God into a rational framework of universal order or law stand in opposition to the biblical trust *(emuna)* that receives only what it receives without demanding that God, man, and world be installed in any objective, comprehensible totality. The security of the former rests on the cosmos that human understanding has opened to it; the "holy insecurity" of the latter on the trust in the reality over against one "that can only properly be addressed and not expressed"—in the meeting with the God whom one can talk *to* but not *about*. Similarly, those who demand a logical, ordered ethics often do so not because they have reason to believe in the objectivity of the moral order, but because they have an almost magic belief that what they posit as fixed, objective, and universal provides security and solidity and protects us against the threat of the irrational and the demonic, the romantic and the Hitlerian. Those who criticize Buber's ethics on this basis complain that if one leaves ethics to the moment and has no a priori values there will be no guide; but they usually leave to one side the all-important problem of the *basis* of moral obligation: the question of whether, in fact, such an objective moral order exists.

Buber's moral philosophy implies that one ever again finds the absolute in the relative—not as a timeless essence or universal, but simply in and inseparable from the unique, the unrepeatable, the new. The reason that the first principle of morality for Buber is hearing and responding is not that the other person is God or contains the essence of God, or "that of God in him," but that he is the creature of God, that the world is God's creation. This is the crucial link between Buber's ethics, his philosophy of religion, and his interpretation of the Bible; for this faithful hearing and responding has only one basic assumption that is not given in the ethics itself—the assumption implicit in creation: reality is not given in me alone or in some selected part of reality with which I identify myself. Everything that confronts me demands my attention and response—whether of love or hate, agreement or opposition to the death—just because it is the reality, and the only reality, that is given me in that moment. The corollary of this presupposition is that there is no thing and no event that is absolutely meaningless or absolutely evil, even though meaninglessness and evil are inescapable components of all human existence. This is the *emuna,* the biblical trust, underlying Buber's ethics. It is the trust that dialogue is the basic and encompassing reality, I-It the secondary and partial one. The ultimate check of the authenticity of an I-Thou relationship is the verification that comes in dialogue itself. Correspondingly, Buber does not *prove* his moral philosophy. Rather, he points to the concrete meeting with the situation in which alone it can be tried and tested. Not only the content of ethics, but also the formal nature and basis of ethics itself must be validated, verified, and authenticated in "the lived concrete."

Greek versus Biblical Ethics

The traditional approach to ethics is Greek; Martin Buber's is biblical. In the *Crito* and *The Republic* the good is intrinsic to a person's being but not to the relations between man and man themselves: one is just, not for the sake of justice, but in order not to injure one's soul. Justice is primarily a reality of the soul rather than of the interhuman. In the Psalms, in contrast, man's very existence is set in a relationship with reality that confronts him, and this relationship transcends "ethics" in the usual understanding of the term:

> The Psalmist has . . . another purpose than the philosopher, who tells us that virtue is its own reward. . . . What he really means is completely untouched by what the philosopher could say to him about the "self-enjoyment" of the moral man. What

he means about the life of the man of whom he speaks cannot be grasped by means of moral values; and what he means about his happiness has its home in another sphere from that of a man's self-satisfaction. Both the conduct of the man's life and his happiness in their nature transcend the realm of ethics as well as that of self-consciousness. Both are to be understood only from a man's intercourse with God.[17]

Here the question of the source of moral obligation is identical with the question of authentic dialogical existence. In this identity all the bases of Buber's ethics join.

6

The Comparative
and the Unique

An Approach to the History
of Religion

In his note to the English edition of his classic work *Religion in Essence and Manifestation,* the distinguished phenomenologist of religion, Gerardius van der Leeuw, expressed regret that he had not been able to incorporate "research of the first order of importance and value" done, since the appearance of the German edition by Martin Buber, Bronislaw Malinowski, and R. R. Marret.[1] What, we might ask, can Buber's approach contribute to the excellent groundwork that has been laid by scholars such as van der Leeuw and my own great teacher, Joachim Wach, to the phenomenological study of the comparative history of religion?

Dialogue and the Unique

At its simplest, we can answer: the understanding of religious symbols, myths, and manifestations as unique products of our dialogue with what Buber calls the "eternal Thou," rather than as divine expression or human projection. So far from being opposites, dialogue and the unique necessarily go together. It is only in dialogue that we can grasp that true uniqueness which is not a product of comparison but of the relation to an event, person, situation, or thing in itself and for its own sake.

At first glance, Buber's emphasis on the uniqueness of the dialogue with the "eternal Thou" might seem incompatible with any approach at all to the comparative history of religion. A second look affords deeper insight. "Comparative" means contrast as well as comparison. Buber uses the category of the "unique" to set limits to the tendency of comparative religonists, from Frazer to Mircea Eliade, to subsume all data under universal patterns or Jungian archetypes. Most of Buber's biblical criticism is of this nature. A third level opens itself to us if we realize that uniqueness and dialogue are corollaries; that the dialogue with the unique in every religion is the prerequisite both to understanding that phenomenon in itself, and to any attempt to subsume it under ideal types and compare it with other phenomena. What we compare are not the phenomena in themselves but the phenomena as we see them.

This is indeed the central message of phenomenology— that the phenomenon is the product of the relation between the seer and the seen, and that we must bracket any supposed objective reality of the phenomenon apart from anyone's knowing it. If Buber is not, in fact, a Husserlian phenomenologist, it is because he is more radical than Husserl in just this respect: namely, that he leaves room for a uniqueness and otherness that Husserl does not: a uniqueness that can only be known in dialogue and of which we cannot speak as it is "in itself." This and nothing else is the meaning of the "eternal Thou," which does not stand for God, or the Absolute, in some metaphysical sense but for our unique dialogue with an Absolute that cannot be known in itself.

In *The Prophetic Faith* Buber states, as a basic principle for his approach to the comparative study of religion, the criterion which he describes as the *uniqueness of the fact.* This criterion must be used carefully and with scientific intuition that seeks after the *concreteness* at the basis of an evidence and thereby approaches the real fact.

> Naturally we do not by this learn the real course of an historic event, but we do learn that in a definite age in a definite circle or tribe or people an actual relationship appeared between the believer and that in which he believes, a unique relationship and according to our perception, at a definite stage too, which also has to be designated unique, a relationship which embodies itself in a concrete event, which continues to operate concretely.[2]

Trust and Faith, Devotio versus Gnosis

Two Types of Faith, the last of Buber's series of books on biblical faith and the origins of messianism, at first appears problematic and even contradictory in the light of Buber's repeated assertions of uniqueness. For here Buber declares that while there are very many contents of faith, there are only two basic forms of faith, a relationship of trust depending upon a contact of my entire being with the one in whom I trust and a relationship of acknowledging, depending upon the acceptance by my entire being of what I acknowledge to be true. What is more, Buber finds the classic example of the former type of faith, which he calls *emuna,* in the early period of Israel; and of the second, which he calls *pistis,* in the early period of Christianity.

He recognizes, to be sure, that the contact in trust leads naturally to the acceptance of what proceeds from the one whom I trust and that the acceptance of the truth acknowledged by me can lead to contact with the one whom it proclaims. "But in the former instance it is the existent contact which is primary, in the latter the acceptance accomplished." He also recognizes here, as with all the typologies he uses in his thought, that in practice the types are mixed. Each of the two types of faith has extended its roots into the other camp. Buber holds, in fact, that in the teachings of Jesus himself, as we know them from the early texts of the gospels, the genuine Jewish principle is manifest, as a result of which the desire of Christians to return to the pure teaching of Jesus has often resulted in an "unconscious colloquy with genuine Judaism."[3]

These qualifications, plus his statement that "every apologetic tendency is far from my purpose," were lost sight of by the many Christian theologians who accused Buber of attacking Christianity. From the other side, Gershom Scholem has designated *Two Types of Faith* as Buber's "weakest book": in part, no doubt, because of the sharpening of the distinction between what Buber later called *devotio* and gnosis.

This typology of "*devotio* versus gnosis" was already implicit at the heart of Buber's Hasidic chronicle-novel *For the Sake of Heaven,* and it stands in close relationship with his contrast between the "prophetic" and the "apocalyptic." But it received its explicit formulation in Buber's dialogue with Rudolf Pannwitz, who, in an essay on Buber's Hasidism, accused Buber of stating the issues between Judaism and Christianity to the disadvantage of the latter. In his reply, Buber disclaimed this specific intention as well as any concern in general with issues of this sort and in so doing set important limits to the proper province of *comparative* religion:

Religions are mansions into which the spirit of man is fit in order that it might not break forth and burst open its world. Each of them has its origin in a particular revelation and its goal in the overcoming of all particularity. Each represents the universality of its mystery in myth and rite and thus reserves it for those who live in it. Therefore, to compare one religion with another, valuing and devaluing, is always an undertaking contrary to being and sense: one's own temple building which can be known from within the innermost shrine compared with the external aspect of the alien temple as it offers itself to the attentive observer.[4]

Emuna and *pistis, devotio* and gnosis Buber sees as ideal types that make it possible to approach the decisive issue *within* Judaism and *within* Christianity.

In the editorial that he wrote for the first issue of *Die Kreatur* in 1926—the journal that broke new ground by being co-edited by a believing Catholic, Protestant, and Jew—Buber said almost the same thing. Borrowing a metaphor from his late friend Florens Christian Rang, Buber described each of the religions as in exile and only God as able to deliver them from this exile. Yet a greeting may come from one house of exile to the other. For the same reason Buber could not agree with his friends Franz Rosenzweig and Hugo Bergmann who spoke of the revelations to Israel and the Church as equally valid. "I stand here before a mystery that I do not know from within, but before which I shudder with awe," said Buber in 1956. "I cannot believe that here something Satanic happened; it is a divine mystery in which we cannot take part." At another time he picture the adherents of the different religions and confessions as climbing on an iceberg that gets smaller at the top. "We are on different sides of this mountain, but it is already given us to see one another from afar."[5]

In one of the fragments on revelation that Buber preserved in his "Gleanings," he elaborated on the metaphor of exile. No religion is a piece of heaven come down to earth. Each represents the relationship of a particular human community as such to the Absolute.

Each religion is a house of the human soul longing for God, a house with windows and without a door; I need only open a window and God's light penetrates; but if I make a hole in the wall and break out, then I have not only become houseless but a cold light surrounds me that is not the light of the living God. Each religion is an exile into which man is driven; . . . in his relationship to God he is separated from the men of other communities; and not sooner than the redemption of the world can we be liberated from the exiles and brought into the common world of God. But the religions . . . call to one another greetings from exile to exile, from house to house through the open windows.[6]

Each religion must renounce its claim to be God's house on earth and content itself with being a house of the men who are turned toward the same purpose of God—a house with windows.

Persons of different faiths can cooperate in the science of religion if they recognize that the divine revelation can never be an object of scientific research but is the reality which limits that research and thereby is its mainstay, its strength-giving origin, and its direction-giving goal. A science of religion which joins itself to a living knowledge about revelation from within this reality can provide a kind of knowledge that the general science of religion cannot provide. But it must do this only in order to be able to penetrate to the unique reality of the other religions and to do it justice. Here, comparing the inner and the outer aspect of one's own religion instructs us how great an exertion of penetration and making imaginatively present is needed in order to come so close to the inner reality of another religion that we can legitmately deal with it scientifically. Here too a boundary is set. "The innermost reality of a religion, its all-holiest and all-realest, is only accessible to the consecrated." This boundary is identical with the mystery of the mutliplicity of the religions.[7]

Hasidism and Zen

In two of his mature essays dealing with the interpretation of Hasidism, Buber attempted just such an imaginative making present of other religions in order to compare them scientifically with Hasidism. In the first, "God and the Soul," Buber makes a legitimate distinction between those theistic mysticisms which preserve the duality of I and Thou and the nontheistic ones that do not, and carries this forward to a significant contrast between the mysticism of Sankara and Meister Eckhart in which the Godhead is removed from human relationship, and that of the Maggid of Mezritch, in which it is precisely the Godhead which enters into relationship with us, as a father limits himself to be able to teach a child.[8]

In the second, "The Place of Hasidism in the History of Religion," Buber undertakes an extended comparison and contrast between Hasidism and a nontheistic mysticism, Zen Buddhism. In reply to Gershom Scholem's criticism of his reliance on Hasidic legends written down 50 years after the formal doctrines, Buber cites Hasidism, Taoism, and Zen as three mysticisms in which the oral legends reveal the life of the mystics more faithfully than the formal teachings. In "The Place of Hasidism," too, Buber juxtaposes Hasidic and Zen tales to show the importance of the present moment, the transmission of the teaching through the central relation between teacher and disciple, and the concern for the particular.

The concern for the particular in Zen, according to Buber, is essentially a way of getting away from intellectualism in order to understand the Buddha nature in oneself; whereas Hasidism is concerned wth the created task of redeeming those people, animals, and things with which one has to do. Hasidism is concerned with what takes place *between* us and the things of this world, Zen with the nonconceptual nature of things as a symbol of the absolute which is superior to all concepts.[9]

The Incomparable and the Kingship of God

The best illustration of the way in which Buber uses the comparative history of religion in order to bring out the uniqueness of the dialogue with the eternal Thou is his study of the origins of messianism in his book *The Kingship of God*. To put forward the idea of a direct theocracy or theopolitical convenant Buber had to range through the whole ancient Oriental treatment of God as King in general and the West Semitic idea of the tribal God, or *malk,* in particular. And he had to do this in the face of the dominant Wellhausen and Mowinckel approaches that used similar comparisons to dissolve any claim to uniqueness on the part of the Hebrew Bible. Buber saw the uniqueness of the divine kingship of Israel not in the development of ideas but "in the three-dimensionality of a living fact of folk history." In the Varuna of the Vedas, in Ahura Mazda of Zoroastrianism, in the divine kingship of Egypt, and still more of Babylon, acknowledgement of a lord took place without there being any actual lordship over the actual community. "Only in ancient Israel, so far as I see, is there—certainly not as a ruling state of mind, but as a clear, manifest tendency of mind advocated wth the passion of the spiritual man—this sublime realism which wants *totally* to deal seriously with faith." This paradox of Israel appears in the pre-state period as the conception of a direct theocracy and in the early-state period as the conception of an indirect, but still genuine theocracy.[10]

Buber bases this claim to uniqueness in part on insight possessed by the general history of religion for a long time, one which "Old Testament scholarship dares not close its eyes to": that the question of origin of a specific piety cannot be derived from another historical sphere where one imagines one need not ask the question of origin.

> For centuries people have wanted to derive the religious achievement which is connected with the name of Moses from Egypt, of whose religion they knew all sorts of things; but the more they discovered about it, the more futile the undertaking proved to be. Since then derivation from the Kenites has taken its place, of whose religion they know nothing at all.[11]

Buber adduces still another principle of the history of religions in conncection with the objection that "the malk-idea stands in indissoluble connection with the naturalistic myth of the ancient Orient, the kingly ideology put forward by the Swedish School, and hence is a nature-mythical schema that contradicts the fundamental essence of the religion of Israel." This principle is a dialectical one of comparison and contrast between individualities and generalities through which, again, the uniqueness of every great religion arises before a background which resembles it typologically but which nevertheless contrasts decisively. "In the concrete process of its origin it is once-for-all and individual, as well as in its concrete appearance; but the incomparable in it can be scientifically grasped only from the point of view of the comparable." The religious traditions of the events themsevles, as visualized in faith, alone makes this eminently historical approach possible.

Buber illustrates the religious tradition of the events themselves from the relation of the God who stands to the wandering host which is his people, or *'am,* in the relationship of leader of its marches, lawgiver, arbitrator and giver of decisions. This *malk*-idea is separated both in its origin and nature from ancient oriental nature mysticism, however many elements it assimilated from its contacts with it in the course of its history:

If an Egyptian, Babylonian, Phoenician god is called 'king', he is called thus either as one of the princes of the gods or also as the highest lord of the state of the gods, in addition doubtless also as Kosmokrator, and then probably also as ruler of the state for which the human kind represents him as his 'son'. In Israel in the sphere of the exodus history JHWH is designated as *melekh,* that is, as the one who goes on ahead of the wandering people; in the mature state He is venerated, to be sure, as the proclaimed world-ruler of heaven and earth and adopts the crown prince as His 'son' and designated regent in Jerusalem, but still in eschatological promise (Micah 2:13) He strides as formerly, along before the delivered bands as *malk.*[12]

Reciprocity of Leader and Led

In connection with the human leader, too, Buber points to "a religio-historical uniqueness in the strictest sense: the ever and again realized, but always intended relation of dialogical exclusiveness between the One who leads and those who are led." Here, too, the divine-dialogue partner of the patriarch or prophet is worshipped by Israel as its *melekh,* its way-determiner. Even where a more historical god, a so-called "bringer of salvation," supplants the preponderantly nature one, as in the Babylonian creation epic in which the gods proclaim Marduk as king before he enters the fight against the powers of the abyss, this is no true parallel; for the reverence is still for a lord of heaven on the part of those cultically bound to him but not also for the heavenly lord of an earthly community of his people.[13]

It is to the Sinai Covenant in particular that Buber points for the unconditioned reciprocity between leader and led which he finds nowhere else in other religions and nowhere else in biblical religion. The sacral-legal act of reciprocity is witnessed in a ceremony between God and man for which none of the parallels adduced by the comparative science of religion offers a real correspondence. In the Bible too only in the Sinai Convenant "is a holy action performed which *institutes sacramentally a reciprocity between the One above and the one below.*" This is not a mere matter of designations. On the contrary, the very heart of religious reality is determined by this difference; for the Cosmic King still leaves the world essentially out of his province whereas the demand of the Kingship of God in Israel is precisely to bring every aspect of life—social, political, economic, communal, family, and personal—under the rule of God.

> The unconditioned claim of the divine Kingship is recongized at the point when the people proclaims JHWH Himself as King, Him alone and directly (Exodus 15:18), and JHWH Himself enters upon the kingly reign (19:6). He is not content to be 'God' in the religious sense. He does not want to surrender to a man that which is not 'God's', the rule over the entire actuality of worldly life: this very rule He lays claim to and enters upon it; for there is nothing which is not God's. He will apportion to the one, for ever and ever chosen by Him, his tasks, but naked power without a situationally related task He does not wish to bestow. He makes known His will first of all as constitution of cult and custom only, also of economy and society—He will proclaim it again and again to the changing generations, certainly but simply as reply to a question, institutionally through priestly mouth, above all, however, in the freedom of His surging spirit, through every one whom His spirit seizes. *The separation of religion and politics which stretches through history is here overcome in real paradox.*[14]

This dialogical exclusiveness in no way means that the God of Israel whom the prophets proclaim as the only God is only the God of Israel. God is God of the peoples, the one who has *led* every wandering people, like Israel, into a "good" land. "Did I not bring Israel out of the land of Egypt—/ and the Philistines form Caphtor / and the Syrians from Kir?" (Amos 9:7). Yet even there where it is explained unmistakably that JHWH is not the God of a tribe, he is proclaimed for ever and ever God of the tribe—"You only have I known." "So strong, so central in JHWH's manifestation is the character of the God walking-on-before, the leading God, the *melekh*."[15]

The Comparative and the Unique

Buber's concern with the comparative *and* with the unique is also central to his book *Moses*. In the Preface to *Moses* Buber holds that what is important is not the familiar category of Monotheism but "the way in which this Unity is viewed and experienced, and whether one stands to it in an exclusive relationship which shapes all other relations and thereby the whole order of life. . . . The universal sun-god of the imperialist 'Monotheism' of Amenhotep IV," wrote Buber in implicit rejection of Freud, "is incomparably closer to the national sun-god of the ancient Egyptian Pantheon than to the God of early Israel, which some have endeavoured to derive from him." The God of Moses is the God of the way, the leader and advance guard who acts at the level of history on the people and between the peoples.[16] Buber claims this same uniqueness for Moses, whose success in wrestling with Pharaoh proves that he is something more than a prophet. "A historical mystery always means a relation between a super-personal fate and a person, and particularly that which is atypical in a person, that by which the person does not belong to his type." Similarly, Israel's acceptance of the Decalogue as its "Constitution" Buber characterizes as "a unique event in human history;" for here only did the decisive process of crystallization of a people come about on a religious basis. "Irrespective of the importance of the typological view of phenomena in the history of the spirit, the latter, just because it is history, also contains the atypical, the unique in the most precise sense." Again, in connection with the scriptural report that the Israelites made the Ark in the wilderness, Buber asserts that "it is a basic law of methodology not to permit the 'firm letter' to be broken down by any general hypothesis based on the comparative history of culture; as long as what is said in that text is historically possible."[17]

Buber's discussion of the God of nature and the God of history in *Moses* is particularly significant because of its dialectical treatment of the comparative and the unique. Already in *The Kingship of God,* in connection with the hypothesis that Moses took over the nature God of his Kenite father-in-law Jethro, Buber observed that neither Israel nor the Kenites is converted to the God of the other: "Israel observes that its folk-God also rules the earthpowers; the Kenites recognize that their mountain or mountain-fire God rescues and guides tribes. The divine image of both grows. Instead of one image which is only a god of nature and one which is only a god of history, there dawns the form of the One who is the lord of nature and the lord of history." In *Moses* Buber puts this on a still broader comparative basis. In the biblical, which is a history religion, there is no Nature in the Greek, the Chinese, or the modern Occidental sense. "What is shown us of Nature is stamped by History. Even the work of creation has a historical tone," especially during the historical period. Later in *Moses* this is stated more subtly and dialectically: "He is the history God, which He is, only when He is not localized in Nature; and precisely because He makes use of everything potentially visible in Nature, every kind of natural existence, for His manifestation."[18] This distinction between the nature God and the God of history Buber ties in with his distinction between the Cosmic King and the *melekh* of Israel:

> The Babylonian divine thrones are nature symbols, that of Israel is a history symbol; and the tablets with the "I" of the God who has led the people out of Egypt are an inseparable part of it. Only in the period of the State, when the theo-political realism succumbed to the influence of the dynastic principle and the Kingdom of YHVH was transfigured and subtilized into a cosmic one lacking all direct binding force, did the nature symbolism prevail; since the aim then was to abstract living history from the domain of the Kingdom of God.[19]

Martin Buber's approach to the comparative history of religion does not seek for some universal essence in metaphysics, experience, or timeless myth, but guards the particularity and the uniqueness of each tradition while bringing them into meaningful connection with one another. The dialogue with the eternal Thou means in every case the wholly concrete event apprehended in the first instance in itself, enregistered in the second in the ideal types which preserve a meaningful dialectic between the general and the particular, and only on the ground of these two instances compared and contrasted with other events, phenomena, and ideal types. Only thus can the comparative history of religion remain both scientific and true to its subject. Only thus can the validity *and* the limitations of comparative scholarship be ascertained in each field and each subject within that field. *This* contribution to the methodology of comparative religion has yet to be adequately taken into account and assessed by today's historians of religion.

7

Dialogue with Oriental Religions

Martin Buber's encounter with Oriental religions is an important one. Until his death he remained actively concerned with comparative mysticism. Although Asian studies was not his great central field of scholarship, he was for years Professor of Comparative History of Religion at the University of Frankfurt and did, in fact, deal in a scholarly manner with Hinduism, Buddhism, and Taoism. His concern with mysticism in Taoism, Hasidism, and Zen, and with Eastern thought, became a steady dialogue; it was an integral part of his path, of his being.

Buber, Herzl, and Tagore

This dialogue, this bringing of himself, made his study of Asian thought and culture neither objective nor subjective and arbitrary. Buber illustrates this with some comments which relate to the meeting of East and West in an essay on "China and Us," an address he gave at a conference on China in 1928 in Heppenheim, where he was living at the time. In this essay he tells about a talk he had with Rabindranath Tagore, the great Hindu philosopher, poet, and, some say, holy man. Tagore raised a question about Zionism. He had always admired the Jewish people, their love of peace, their scholarship, but he felt that there was a great danger that the establishing of a Jewish homeland in Palestine might result in too great an influence of Western ways. What he wanted instead was to see Palestine more in the image of the East as he saw it, that is, minus the industrialism of the West.

Buber was not unsympathetic to this view. On the contrary, Buber tells how in 1901, as editor of *Die Welt,* the official Zionist journal of Theodor Herzl, he met with Herzl in the Zionist Central Bureau in Vienna to discuss his editorial activities. On the wall of the room where they met hung the new Palestine relief map which had just reached the bureau. After a brief greeting, Herzl led Buber at once to the map and began to point out to him the economic and technical future of the land. His finger glided over the deserts and there were terraced settlements; it glided over an empty plain and there arose in powerful rows the factories of a hundred industries; it led over the Bay of Haifa, and, through the force of his words, Buber beheld the "future port of Asia." Finally his finger returned to the Jordan, and Herzl recited to him the plan to erect a mightly dam that with its energy would supply the total economic life of the land. And now his finger tapped on a point of the map, and he cried: "How much horsepower has Niagara? Eight million? We shall have ten million!" Buber stood entranced before this magic work. He felt how the Jordan-Niagara Falls sprayed over him, and at the same time he had to smile: how remote that was, how unreal! No, it was not for that, thought the young man, that we served; not to take part in the Americanization of Asia had we inscribed Zion's name on our banner. God be thanked that this was only a dream!

Only long afterward, many years after Herzl's death, did it become clear to Buber that at that time it was Herzl—and not he—who had meant the real Palestine. For Buber, at that time, it was *"das geliebte und gelobte"*—the beloved and the Promised Land that had to be won anew, the land of the soul and of the message, the land in which the miracle of redemption should reach fulfillment. For Herzl, in contrast, it was a wholly particular land with wholly particular geographical and geological characteristics, and, therefore, also with clearly determinable technical possibilities which he not only knew but also beheld.

Does this mean, asks Buber, that the choice is inescapable between the maximum possible horsepower on the one hand and the way toward redemption on the other? No, and this, too, Buber confesses to learning only many years later. If Asia cannot escape going the way of Europe and America, technicalization may still be kept as a means and not allowed to become an end. This means a limit should be set to technical progress, precisely at the point where it injures the unity and the truth of life.[1]

Buber felt that what Tagore had said was said in a heartfelt manner. But he believed that it was removed from the reality of the situation. Buber pictured to himself a man who proposed to erect a great symbol on the top of a mountain and who was carrying it all the way to the top. Should someone say to this man that he could get to the top much faster without the symbol, he could only reply that his whole purpose of going to the mountaintop was to take the symbol there. Buber maintained that the same is true of the industrial civilization of the West. We carry it and it carries us. It is not that Buber did not see the evils of that civilization; he just did not think it was possible to throw it out and go backward. When he looked at the development of Japan and India, he doubted that even they could be spared a similiar route.

In the face of this situation, Buber asks, "What can China have to say to us today?" Here he makes an important distinction about dialogue that shows that it is not a matter of arbitrary selectivity. We cannot take over Chinese art or wisdom in the sense in which the eighteenth century took the art of engraving and turned it into a very charming chinoiserie. Nor can we take over the noble sayings of Confucius and treat them as universal. That, Buber says, is the real sin against the spirit. The real receiving can only take place as the receiving of a living reality with the forces of one's own life. How does one receive such a reality? Buber holds that every genuine culture has had, not an idea, but an image of man which is the human standing above it. It is only from our situation and our dialogue with that image that we can receive from the unique reality embodied in every culture.

Buber and the Mystical

Neither Hinduism nor Buddhism remains a central part of Buber's later thought as do Taoism, Hasidism, and Zen, but they play an important part in his early developmental thinking. The distinguished American philosopher W. T. Stace accomplished the remarkable feat of remaining a naturalist philosopher, while in the later part of his life becoming a mystic close to the spirit of Aldous Huxley's *Perennial Philosophy*. In his book on *Mysticism and Logic,* Stace refers to the famous story of the conversion that Buber tells in "Dialogue" *(Between Man and Man)* and *Meetings*. In this story Buber relates how he gave up his tendency to mystic ecstasy after he found he was not really present for a young man who, in despair, had come to see him, and was later, out of that same despair, killed in the first world war. Stace explains this in terms of there being no mysticism in Judaism, and from this error he deduces the explanation for Buber's critique of mysticism. This is exactly the reverse of the truth in at least three respects. First, there is a mysticism in Judaism. Second, as Buber has often said, it is the events in one's life, for example, the first world war in his own, which really bring decisive change in one's thought, and not actual cultural influences. But third, Buber was concerned with Hinduism before he became concerned with Hasidism and Jewish mysticism. In a 1901 essay on the great German mystic Jacob Boehme, Buber quotes Ludwig Feuerbach's statement that the meeting between men—between I and Thou—is God, only to state that we are closer to St. Franics and still closer to the Vedānta. He may not have understood the Vedānta fully at that point, because he was very concerned with the I, but nontheless, he explicit rejected I and Thou in favor of the unity of the I.

Three years later Buber came into close contact with Hasidism, a form of popular communal Jewish mysticism, and he spent a lifetime interpreting and retelling its legends and stories. The first important product of his withdrawal from Zionist political activity to the study of Hasidism was his book, *The Tales of Rabbi Nachman.* In his next book, *The Legend of the Baal Shem* (1908), he speaks not only of ecstasy but also of a communal mysticism of joy and service and of love and humility as the reality found between person and person. In the Preface, he speaks of legend as "the myth of I and the Thou," the first place where he explicitly spoke of I and Thou in a positive way. Yet, in 1909, the very next year, Buber brought out a book called *Ecstatic Confessions,* as far as I know the first mystical anthology. It included many Christian Western mystics, but it also included Sri Ramakrishna and the whole range of Eastern mysticism. In the Introduction, entitled "Ecstasy and Confession," Buber takes a Vedāntist position in striking contrast to what he had said of Hasidism:

Not suspecting that the poor individual "I" contains the "World I," most mystics have connected their experience with God, and have made of it a multiform mystery. Only in the primitive word of India is the "I" proclaimed that is one with the "All" and with the "One." The unity which the mystic experiences when he has brought all his former multiplicity into Oneness is not a relative unity, for the ecstatic man no longer has outside of himself others with whom he has community. It is the absolute, unlimited Oneness which includes all others.

That is clearly a nondualistic statement. In 1910 at the first German sociological conference, Ernst Troelsch attempted to introduce mysticism as a different type of religious social grouping than church, denomination, and sect. Buber rejected this attempt on the grounds that the mystic in his ecstasy knows no communal or social reality; he stands in isolated relation to God. In "Ecstasy and Confession," however, Buber speaks of the paradox that all mystics want to communicate, and in so doing enter the reality of the I and the Thou, the Many and the One. "We turn inward and listen, and we do not know which sea it is that we hear." Buber was closer here to the qualified nondualist position of Ramānuja than to Sankara, even though he was seemingly referring to Sankara and unqualified nondualism.

Mystical Experience and Mystical Philosophy

In the book, *Daniel,* written in 1913, Buber refers to the Vedānta umistakably, though, not by name, as one of the false paths that we can take on the way to the "final teaching." *Daniel* was not Buber's final teaching, but he imagined it was. But the experience of this wrong path confirms that the unity that was found outside the world can be won again in the world. In *I and Thou* (1923), where he arrived at his mature philosophy, Buber speaks of two teachings of mystic union, one of absorption, as in the Gospel of John, and the other of identity, as in the Vedānta. He rejects the philosophies underlying these two teachings without denying the mystical experience itself, which he reinterprets as either the soul's becoming whole and one, or as the person meeting the Thou with such intensity that in that meeting both I and Thou are forgotten. Buber criticizes the tendency of many mystics to turn mystic experience into a mystic philosophy and proclaim either a monism or a nondualism. This does not mean that Buber's mature philosophy is a dualistic one, as Stace and many others imagine. *I and Thou* does not fit either of the two categories, dualist and nondualist. Yet there is a decisive change here that goes along with Buber's almost ascetic renunciation of his own natural tendency to ecstasy. For he refers to these as "phenomena of the brink" and declares that sunlight on a sprig of maple is closer to our lived life than all ecstasies. In *The Spirit of Orient and Judaism,* written in 1916, he contrasts a Greco-Western emphasis upon stasis and the visual with a general Asian spirit of movement and dynamism, and he includes Judaism in this Asian tendency.

Buber's Affinity with Taoism

Buber's relation with Taoism is more complex. Taoism, Hasidism, and Zen, I would claim, are three mysticisms of the "particular," which give the lie to the Perennial Philosophy that there is some one essence in all of mysticism. At the very end of my long monograph on "Buber's Encounter with Mysticism,"[2] I tell how a Zen master visited Buber in Jerusalem with an American disciple. While the Zen master remained silent, the American disciple talked volubly to Buber and explained that there was one essence of all mysticism. When Buber asked somewhat sternly, "And what is that essence?" the Zen master got up and vigorously shook Buber's hand! Buber, in any case, did not believe in that type of comparison that leaves out the uniqueness of each religion. He was a pupil of Wilhelm Dilthey, whose phenomenology left room for the unique. He certainly understood and utilized the typological method. But he also believed that you had to know each phenomenon in its uniqueness, and quarreled with that aspect of comparative religion that looks only for resemblances.

The influence of Taoism came relatively early in Buber's thought, and unlike the Vedānta persisted in his mature thought. While on the one hand Buber seemed to reject some aspects of Taoism that he had earlier espoused, on the other this dialogue with Taoism remained of central importance to him throughout his life. Buber's long essay on "The Teaching of the Tao," published in 1911, as an afterword to the *Parables of Chuang-tzu,* had a great impact on the German Youth Movement. Buber was one of the idols of German youth, not because of what he wrote on Hasidism, but because of this publication of Chuang-tzu and his essay "The Teaching of the Tao." In this essay Buber was not concerned so much with metaphysical thought as with being as embodied in what he calls the "central man." In this connection he dealt with Lao-tzu, whose path he saw as pointing to the "perfected" or "completed" man—an image of the human which cannot be spelled out or analyzed. He compared this way many times to the Heraclitean Logos, and to Heraclitus, whose sense of the opposites was close to the yin and yang of the Tao. Each thing reveals the Tao through its unity of existence, he declared. Thus the Tao is found only in the manifoldness of all things. Here we have unmistakably the mysticism of the particular and the concrete.

In the introduction to his book *Hinweise,* for the most part the German original of *Pointing the Way,* Buber said that he only included in these "hints" those essays that he could still stand behind. When I translated *Pointing the Way,* I declared to Buber that he could not fully stand behind "The Teaching of the Tao," because it speaks of a unity which he went beyond in *I and Thou.* "You are right," Buber replied. "Yet I have to include this essay as an indispensable part of my way. I had to go through this encounter with mysticism in general and the Tao, in particular, to reach my own independent thought." And his independent thought bears important traces of Taoism without the concept of unity.

In "The Teaching of the Tao," Buber wrote,

> The Tao is the path of things, their manner, their peculiar order, but it exists as such in things only potentially. It comes out only in the contact with others. Then it becomes active. If there were metal and stone without Tao, there would be no sound. They would have the power of sound, but it does not come out of them if they are not struck. Thus it is with all things.[3]

So the Tao of things only becomes actual and manifest through contact with the world of the perfected man. Here is a clear presentiment of Buber's mature philosophy of dialogue. All creating, from the point of view of this teaching, means nothing more than to call forth the Tao of the world.

The Live Encounter

One of the things that is most puzzling to Westerners who come to Buber's thought, including many Christian theologians whom it has deeply influenced, is that Buber keeps insisting that there can be an I-Thou relation with trees and cats and stones. He does not mean that the tree is a dryad that winks at you as you go by, but that there can be some active reciprocal contact. In a book of Thomas Merton's called *The Way of Chuang Tzu,* there is a story called "The Wood Carver," which is not only a remarkable representation of the philosophy of meeting, but actually explains one of the most obscure parts of *I and Thou.* In *I and Thou,* Buber says there are three types of I-Thou relations: the I-Thou with nature, the I-Thou with fellow men, and the I-Thou with "spiritual essences." The German original of this Platonic-sounding phrase was *geistige Wesenheiten.* What Buber meant was nothing Platonic at all. He was speaking about art. The sculptor looks at the marble, let's say. He does not see the finished form in it as yet; he meets its possibility, and the form is a product of that meeting. I know a fine sculptor who went to Vermont to get a particularly hard marble. She needed that encounter with it in order to produce what she did. This sense of meeting is very clear in Michelangelo's "Prisoners" in Florence; they are not fully carved out of the stone, so that we can see the meeting between Michelangelo and the marble in the very process of emerging into form.

In the story of the wood-carver, as Merton retells it, Khing, the master carver, made a bell stand of precious wood. When it was finished, everyone who saw it was astounded, and they said it must be the work of spirits. When the Prince of Lu said to the master carver, "What is your secret?" Khing replied,

> I am only a workman. I have no secret. There is only this: When I began to think about the work you commanded, I guarded my spirit, did not expend it on trifles that were not to the point. I fasted in order to set my heart at rest. After three days fasting, I had forgotten gain and success. After five days I had forgotten praise and criticism. After seven days I had

forgotten my body with all its limbs. By this time all the thought of your Highness and of the court faded away. All that might distract me from the work had vanished. I was collected in a single thought of the bell stand. Then I went to the forest to see the trees in their own natural state. When the right tree appeared before my eyes, the bell stand also appeared in it, clearly, beyond doubt. All I had to do was to put forth my hand and begin. If I had not met this particular tree, there would have been no bell stand at all.[4]

Buber says in *The Knowledge of Man* that the sculpture is neither the expression of the human soul, nor the impression of a natural object, but that it is the meeting between the world of man and the world of things. "What happened?" replies the wood-carver. "My own collected thought encountered the hidden potential in the wood. From this live encounter came the work which you ascribe to the spirits." This is one remarkable example of Buber's affinity with Taoism.

The Action of the Whole Being

The second is the whole concept of the *wu wei,* sometimes misunderstood in the West as nonaction. It is nonaction only in the sense that it is not the Western type of action. It is not the action which intervenes and interferes. It is the action of the whole being. In "The Teaching of the Tao," Buber spends a good deal of time contrasting two types of action, the one which interferes in the web of things, and the other which, instead of interfering, rests in the work of the inner deed, but is an effecting of the whole, where things happen as you will them, and yet you seem to be doing nothing, where you rule people and yet they do not know that they are ruled. He relates this to the will, the willing person. There is no longer any division between him and what is willed. What is willed becomes being. The perfected man does not interfere in the life of things, he does not impose himself on them, but helps all beings to their freedom. Through his unity he leads them to *the* unity, he liberates their nature and their destiny, he releases Tao in them. In the life together of human beings, the ruler rules in the same way. He guards and unfolds the natural life of the kingdom. To do this he does not use violence; he just makes a gesture with his hand. What he wants to happen happens, and yet the people think they are ruling themselves. This is indeed what is said in the teaching of Lao-tzu. The real ruler takes all the suffering of others on himself; he bears the country's need and pain; that is what it means to be the kingdom's king. This is very similar to a Hasidic story that Buber retells. Moshe Leib of Sasov learned to love by coming to an inn where he heard one drunken peasant ask another, "Do you love me?" "Certainly I love you," replied the second. "I love you like a brother." But the first shook his head and insisted. "You don't love me. You don't know what I lack. You don't know what I need." The second fellow fell into sullen silence, but Moshe Leib said, "But I understood. To love another is to know his need and bear the burden of his pain and his sorrow." "The true ruler liberates the individual from this dominion of the multitude," says Lao-tzu, or in Buber's words, "He makes the crowd no longer a crowd." That is one of the most important sentences in Buber's later thought. In criticizing Søren Kierkegaard who says, "The crowd is untruth," Buber says, "Our task is to make the crowd not bundled, but bound," to "de-crowd the crowd."

There are other passages, to be sure, where Buber seems to be abjuring Taoism. For example, in *Daniel* (1913), he refers to the nondifferentiation of the opposites in what is clearly a reference to Taoism. Important as it is in getting a glimpse of the whole, this nondifferentiation is still not the fullness of real life, Daniel says. At the end of "The Teaching of the Tao," Buber compares Heraclitus and Lao-tzu at length, where there are many extremely interesting resemblances of the harmony of opposites, the tension of the bow and the lyre, the yin and the yang. Forty-five years later in the essay "What Is Common to All" (in *The Knowledge of Man*), Buber speaks of the tendency of modern man to flee into collectivism or into individualism in order to escape from the true human task of building the common cosmos through the common logos, creating and adding onto the common world through common speech-with-meaning. To Buber, Heraclitus' injunction to follow the common is of the essence, yet he uses a Taoist story to illustrate the opposite. This is the legend of a country where people are asleep for 6 months of the year and are awake for 6 months of the year. It is when they are asleep, the Taoist legend implies, that they are in the true reality. Buber also recounts in this connection the famous story about Chuang-tzu, who dreamt he was a butterfly, and when he awoke he was not sure whether he was Chuang-tzu who had dreamt he was a butterfly or a butterfly dreaming that he was Chuang-tzu. For all that, the evidence is overwhelming that Taoism remains extremely important in Buber's thought.

A Reality that Works in the Depths of History

In "China and Us" (1928)[5] Buber states that while he does not think that Confucianism, with its reverence for the ancestors, has much to teach the West, there is something that China has to give us, namely, the Taoist teaching of *wu wei*, the nonaction which is really the action of the whole being. He says that we have begun to learn that success is of no consequence. We have begun to learn that the really powerful existence does not yield historical success:

it endures across generations, making its way underneath the surface of historical fashion. We have begun to learn this in a negative and downright foolish manner. But there where we stand, or there where we shall soon stand, we shall directly touch upon the reality from which Lao-tzu spoke. This statement was made 5 years before Hitler came to power in Germany.

It is particularly significant that there is an exact parallel here to what Buber himself does with the notion of the "suffering servant" in Deutero-Isaiah, and also in his Hasidic chronicle-novel, *For the Sake of Heaven*: namely, that the hidden reality which works in the depths of history may be the truly powerful one. In "The Cause and the Person" (from his autobiographical fragments, *Meetings*) Buber tells of a friend who found himself in conflict with Theodor Herzl at a Zionist congress. Herzl had publicly wronged this man, who was a member of the Democratic Fraction to which Buber belonged, and there was no way to undo the wrong. Buber asks, "Might there not be yet another reality, different from that of obvious world history—a reality hidden and powerless because it has not yet come into power?" Might there be "men with a mission who have not been called to power and yet are, in essence, men who have been summoned?" Is success the only criterion? Is there perhaps a "dark charisma" which confirms the man who is accorded no historical success, whose success is anonymous, who perhaps does not have any success? The parallel between "China and Us" and "The Cause and the Person," both written within the same year, is striking.

The Free Person versus the Self-Willed Person

We cannot understand Buber's central work to which his thought led, and from which the rest came, namely, *Ich und*

Du, I and Thou, unless we understand the Taoist concept of *wu wei.* If we look at Part Two of *I and Thou,* we discover that everything that Buber says about the free man who wills without arbitrariness is, in fact, the direct application in almost the same words of what he wrote in "The Teaching of the Tao" about the perfected man of the Tao; and the contrast with the man who intervenes and wants to *make* things happen is also the same. The free man is he who wills without arbitrary self-will. He believes in reality, the real solidarity; he believes in destiny and that it stands in need of him. He knows he must go out to the meeting with the other with his whole being. The matter will not turn out according to his decision, but what is to come will come only when he decides from his genuine ability to will. He must sacrifice his puny, unfree will, controlled by things and instincts, to his grand will, which sets out to find destined being. Then he intervenes no more, but at the same time, he does not merely let things happen. He listens to what is emerging from himself, to the course of being in the world—not in order to be supported by it, but in order to bring it to reality as it desires and has need of him with the human spirit in deed, human life, and death.

The man of I-It is really the anti-*wu wei* man; he is the self-willed man who has no trust but wants to *make* things happen. He wants to effectuate them. This is the exact same contrast Buber makes in "Elements of the Interhuman" *(The Knowledge of Man)* between the educator and the propagandist. The educator does not have a truth, but he trusts that the seed sown in the soul of the other will spring to light in its own way. The propagandist has no trust, and so he wants to manipulate through loudspeakers to make the thing happen as he wills it. The anti-*wu wei* man has no grand will, only a self-will which he passes off as a real will. The unbelieving core in the self-willed man can perceive nothing but unbelief and self-will, establishing a purpose, and devising a means, the means here and the end there. When in thought he turns to himself, he knows this. So he spends most of his time turning his thoughts away from himself. This can lead only to that despair, that wisdom of foolishness which comes when the I-It man reaches the bottom; and *then* we have the beginning of the turning toward real meeting.

The Wordless Depths

In "The Wordless Depths" section of "Dialogue" *(Between Man and Man),* Buber says he knows from his unforgettable experience that there is a state in which the bonds of the personal nature of life seem to have fallen away from us, and we experience an undivided unity. "But I do not know what the soul willingly imagines and indeed is bound to imagine, that in this I had attained to a union with the primal being or the Godhead. This is an exaggeration no longer permitted to responsible understanding." What is permitted to responsible understanding, Buber suggests, is a recognition of an undifferentiated prebiographical unity hidden beneath all biographical change, development, and complication of the soul. In experiencing that unity, we naturally experience nothing else. We experience an absence of all otherness. "But in the actual reality of lived life, the man at such a moment is not above but beneath the creaturely situtation," says Buber, "the situation which is mightier and truer than all ecstasies."

The Buddha

The enormous influence of Taoism upon Zen makes it not surprising that Buber later became interested in Zen Buddhism. Although it did not have a lasting impact on his thought, Buber was interested in Buddhism per se at least as early as Taoism. His little essay on "Buddha" written in 1908, or earlier, is striking precisely for its total deemphasis on historical Buddhism, something for which he later, mistakenly, criticized Zen. The Buddha enlarged the ground of the Vedānta, not with an idea but with a deed. He rejected all positions and negations, refused all solutions of antinomies for the sake of the "Path." The Buddha is the Prometheus of India whose deed has no expansion in space and no duration in time. His deed is not effected; it grows out of the moment, out of eternity. Like Siddhartha, the hero of Hermann Hesse's novel by that name, Buber separated himself from those around Gautama but not from him.

The Buddha-word for the parthenogenesis of the soul is: return, reincarnation. The mother of the deed is the deed of an earlier life. The knowing of a Gautama is a being. Buddha beholds the things, is the things, beholds the world, is the world. His negation, his refusal is nothing other than the completed, perfected being. The perfected being is the end and the bliss and its own limit and the Nothing. It is the fulfilled deed. "Asia speaks. Not the historical-geographical category 'Asia.' It is the voice that receives us in the refuge of the primal words. It does not instruct. It protects, it comforts, it heals."[6]

Almost 15 years later in *I and Thou,* the classic statement of his mature philosophy of dialogue, Buber once again speaks of the Buddha's "noble silence" about metaphysical questions, which has its theoretical base in the fact that fulfillment is beyond the categories of thought and expression and its practical base in the fact that such questions do not contribute to a life of salvation. "The primal conditon of salvation is undivided confrontation of the undivided mystery." Like all true teachers he does not wish to impart an opinion, but to teach the "way." He denies only the assertion that man cannot walk in the way and asserts only that Unborn, Uncreated, Unformed without which there would be no way. But the mature Buber rejects the goal of the cessation of pain and release from the cycle of births.

> If we did know that there is reincarnation we would not seek to escape it, and we would long not indeed for gross being but for the power to speak in each existence in its own way and language, the eternal *I* that perishes, and the eternal *Thou* that is imperishable.

The Buddha's becoming aware of the events in our body is almost the opposite of our physical insight with its certainty about the sense. "And he does not lead the united being further to that highest saying of *Thou* that is accessible to it. His innermost decision seems to rest on the extinction of the ability to say *Thou*." Buber recognized, of course, that the Buddha knows the saying of the *Thou* to men, as in his direct speaking to his disciples. But he does not teach it. He certainly knows too, in the silent depths of his being, the saying of *Thou* to the primal reality. This act, too, is a relational event that has taken on substance, a repsonse to the *Thou*. But about this response the Buddha reserves silence. In *I and Thou* Buber places a value on historical Buddhism that he had denied in "Buddha": The Buddha's succession among the peoples, the "great vehicle," contradicted him magnificently by addressing the eternal human *Thou* under the name of Buddha himself. "And it awaits as the coming Buddha, the last of this world age, him who shall fulfill love."[7] Thus we can only follow the Buddha so far and no further without being disloyal to "Real life is meeting."

More than a quarter of a century later in his essay on "Religion and Philosophy" in *Eclipse of God* Buber used the Buddha to illustrate his paradoxical concept of the

"Absolute Person" and its corollary, the assertion that "the personal manifestation of the divine is not decisive for the genuineness of religion." The Greek philosopher Epicurus teaches that there are gods—immortal and perfect beings who live in the spaces between the worlds without power over the world or interest in it—gods whom we should worship through images and rites though they take no notice of us. "Here," Buber states, "is a kind of dogma and also a cultic practice, and yet clearly a philosophical rather than a religious attitude." Buddha, in contrast, treats the gods of popular belief, so far as he deigns to mention them at all, with calm and considered good will, not unmixed with irony. One may worship them, but *they* pay homage to the "Awakened One," freed and freeing from the wheel of births. But Buddha also knows a genuinely divine, an "Unborn, Unoriginated, Uncreated," if only in this wholly negative designation about which he refuses to make any further assertion. "Yet he stands related to it with his whole being. Here is neither proclamation nor worship of a deity, yet unmistakable religious reality." What is decisive for the genuineness of religion is that I relate myself to the divine as to Being which is over against me, though *not* over against me *alone*.[8]

Hasidism and Zen: Mysticisms of the Particular

Buber encountered Zen Buddhism in its texts, in the writings of D.T. Suzuki, and in sporadic meetings with Zen masters and students, including Suzuki himself whom I brought together with him in New York in 1951. In Buber's essay, "The Place of Hasidism in the History of Religions" (*The Origin and Meaning of Hasidism,* 1960), the major contrast is between Hasidism and Zen. This essay bears out my assertion that both Hasidism and Zen, like Taoism, are mysticisms of the particular. They do not rest on the bond of the Absolute with the Universal, or the general. In his essay on "Religion and Philosophy" *(Eclipse of God)*, Buber says that philosophy tends to be the bond between the Absolute and the general, whereas religion is the bond between the Absolute and the particular. When I asked him about the Hindu Vedānta, he replied that Hindu philosophy is one thing, but lived experience is another.

In "The Place of Hasidism in the History of Religion" Buber tells how, after the death of Rabbi Moshe of Kobryn, one of his disciples was asked, "What was the most important thing to your master?" He thought for a while and said, "Whatever he happened to be doing at the moment." Then Buber quotes a Zen question, "What is the word that saves, the word that wipes out the sin of millions of eons?" to which the Zen master's answer is, "What is right under your nose!"

In both Hasidism and Zen, the teacher is the person who, through immediate contact with the disciple, transmits the message intact. Buber says, "I know of no two religions comparable to Hasidism and Zen in which the transmission from generation to generation is so important. And this teaching is very often not merely some objective handing over, but rather very personal." In the Hasidic tale which Buber entitles, "Not to Say Torah but to Be Torah" *(The Early Masters)*, Rabbi Leib, the son of Sara, says, "I went to the Maggid of Mezritch not to hear him say Torah but to see him lace and unlace his felt boots." Buber cites the closely parallel Zen story of the man who complained that he served the master for 3 years without receiving any spiritual instruction. The master responds in surprise, "How can you say that you received no spiritual instruction? When you brought me tea, did I not take it? When you bowed, did I not bow?" Truth in both, Buber says, is not found in a content of a teaching, but in human existence itself. And the relation between teacher and disciple is central.

The Contrast between Hasidism and Zen

Then Buber comes to the contrast between Hasidism and Zen, and this is subtler and less evident. He suggests that Hasidism is the one mysticism in which history remains important, the one mysticism where the seemingly incompatible spheres of revelation and illumination do meet. Zen Buddhism, in contrast, although it is a part of Māhāyana Buddhism, which is historical, is itself largely nonhistorical. He elaborates on the nature of Zen as a mysticism of the particular by quoting such statements as "This earth is the Pure Land of the Lotus, this body is the body of the Buddha," and "Nirvāna is Saṁsāra." Nonetheless, according to Buber, the concern for the particular in Zen is essentially a way of getting away form intellectualism. It is a way of understanding the Buddha nature in oneself.

Hasidism, in contrast, is concerned with uplifting the fallen sparks to their divine source, with the created task of redemption of those people, animals, and things with which one has to do. Buber understands, of course, that the Zen Buddhist is not concerned with "salvation." But in Hasidism it really is a matter of a redemption that takes place between us and the things. Hasidism says that God is in our prayers, that God is prayer. But it does not see God as the substance of the soul. Even the relationship of the most intimate reciprocity remains a relationship. Even the most personal mysticism rests in the shadow of the historical revelation. Even the most personal teaching arises out of the bond of the historical teaching. In Israel, all religion is history, including mystical religion.

Zen diverts the knowledge of the transcendent from discursive thought. The things themselves do not matter, but their nonconceptual nature is a symbol of the absolute which is superior to all concepts. In Hasidism, Buber suggests, the things themselves do matter, for it is a mysticism in which time is hallowed.[9] It is ironic that one of the attacks that Scholem makes on Buber is precisely on this point. He claims that the Hasidism were interested in the particular only to nullify it, that they really were Gnostics and Neo-Platonists concerned with the Transcendent.[10] Buber's response to this, which Scholem does not respond to, is that there were two streams within Hasidism—one, that of the founder, the Baal Shem Tov, in which the hallowing of the everyday for its own sake is emphasized; the other, that of his great disciple the Maggid of Mezritch, in which the particular is mainly of importance as a stage of a dialectical process in which it is finally nullified in order to reach the transcendent. In his writings on Hasidism (with the exception of his chronicle-novel, *For the Sake of Heaven*), Buber did not emphasize this second stream. In this, Scholem's criticism is partially justified, for many people in the Western world took their understanding of Hasidism from Buber, just as they used to rely solely on the interpretations of D. T. Suzuki for their understanding of Zen. What is not justifiable is Scholem's failure, after his chapter on "Hasidism" in *Major Trends in Jewish Mysticism,* which agrees in all central respects with Buber, ever to acknowledge that the first stream existed at all. Instead, he urged his readers to dismiss Buber's interpretation of Hasidism as entirely invalid.[11]

There is one point in which I myself must criticize Buber's contrast between Hasidism and Zen. I agree that Hasidism is set in the historical tradition of redemption as opposed to individual salvation or enlightenment. But I cannot fully agree with what Buber says about Zen focusing on discovering that Buddha nature within oneself. The Buddha nature is not just inside oneself. It is in all things— a nondual duality which is simultaneously the One and the ten thousand things. In this respect I find Hasidism closer to Zen that Buber does, though this nondual duality is still not *dialogue* with the other in its otherness, as in Buber's philosophy and his interpretation of Hasidism.

Religion is often taken to be a movement away from mundane reality to the spirit floating above it. Zen Buddhism says no such movement is possible: there is only the one spirit-sense reality. It says, secondly, that it is our reason that has created the impression that there are these separate worlds of spirit and sense-intellect. This differs strikingly from the Hindu Vedānta with its statement that this world is *maya,* or illusion, and that Brahman is reality. Instead, we have the remarkable statement that the "One" and the "ten thousand things" are identical, that "nirvana *is* samsāra." It is our minds that bifurcate existence into body and spirit, the one and the many. We cannot overcome our existential dilemma by fleeing from the many to the one; for this very attempt to overcome dualism leads us to still another dualism—that of the one as opposed to the many. One must instead go right to the concrete particular which at the same time is the Buddha Nature. There is no process here of abstracting from concrete reality, or uncovering the essence and shucking off this world. There is no Hindu *nama-rupa*—no world of name and form which is to be understood as merely that, and therefore illusion. On the contrary, the very particularity of things, their very name and form is the only means through which one can attain enlightenment. A Japanese Zen woman goes out and sees the morning-glory vine on the bucket she means to draw water from. She goes to the next farm for her water and writes a haiku: "Oh morning glory with bucket made captive, I beg for water." She and the morning glory are one, the distance is overcome, but in a very specific manner. It is not as if there were one essence or absolute that could be abstracted from the two apart from their particularity. The particularity is preserved.

Zen is just the everyday life—pulling up carrots in the garden, peeling potatoes in the kitchen.

Walking is Zen, sitting is Zen. Whether talking or remaining silent, whether moving or standing quiet, the essence itself is ever at ease.

One finds the "essence" just as much in the movement of the world as in the nonmovement. In that sense, Zen is like Taoism: it does not cling to one opposite or the other.

Straight runs the path of non-duality and non-trinity. Abiding with the no-particular which is in particulars, Whether going or returning, they remain for ever unmoved. . . . This very earth is the lotus land of purity, And this body is the body of the Buddha.

The Buddha Nature, the particulars, and the no-particulars are all one reality.

When D.T. Suzuki once came to Sarah Lawrence College to speak to our Philosophy Seminar, there was a Hindu woman from my class in the History of Religions who joined us at supper beforehand. "Do you believe that God is in the sugar bowl?" Suzuki asked her. "Yes," she replied, and he rejoined, "So do we." "Do you believe that God is in you?" he pursued. "Yes," she again replied, and he again assented, "So do we." But then he asked her, "Do you believe the same God is in the sugar bowl and in you?" This time when she said Yes, he countered, "That is where we differ!" It is not the same God, even though it is not a different one. It is neither two nor one. The Buddha Nature is to be comprehended in and through birth-and-death, and birth-and-death must somehow harbor the Buddha Nature in it. Nirvana *is* samsāra.[12]

Analysis and Reality

In *The Knowledge of Man* Buber asserts that the perception of one's fellow man as a whole, as a unity, and as unqiue is opposed by the analytical, reductive, and deriving look between man and man that dominates in our time.

This look is analtyical, or rather pseudo-analytical, since it treats the whole being as put together and therefore able to be taken apart—not only the so-called unconscious which is accessible to relative objectification, but also the psychic stream itself, which can never, in fact, be grasped as an object. This look is a reductive one because it tries to contract the manifold person, who is nourished by the microcosmic richness of the possible, to some schematically surveyable and recurrent structures. And this look is a deriving one because it supposes it can grasp what a man has become, or even is becoming, in genetic formulae, and it thinks that even the dynamic central principle of the individual in this becoming can be represented by a general concept. An effort is being made today radically to destroy the mystery between man and man. The personal life, the ever near mystery, once the source of the stillest enthusiasms, is levelled down.[13]

Similarly, there is much in both Zen Buddhism and Taoism which raises serious questions about the assumption of most of the intellectual currents of the nineteenth and twentieth centuries that *analysis* is the way to reach reality. If I assume that all things are really reducible to their component parts, that means I have already found what I believe to be the basic reality—whether it be Marxist dialectic, economic determinism, Freud's or Jung's theory of the libido, or the analytical categories of the linguistic philosopher. Lao-tzu, in contrast, defines sanity as not wanting to measure the measureless, untouchable source of reality; and Zen says that if you begin to reason about the substance you see before you, you at once fall into the error.

It is like the boundless void which cannot be fathomed or measured. This universal mind alone is the Buddha and there is no distinction between the Buddha and sentient beings. . . . You have but to recognize that *real mind is expressed in these perceptions, but is not dependent on them on the one hand, nor separate from them on the other.* . . . You should refrain from seeking universal mind apart from them or abandoning them in your pursuit of the Dharma. . . for there is nowhere in which the Way cannot be followed. (Italics added)

Martin Buber in *I and Thou* has a remarkably similar passage in which he says: "If you explore the life of things and of conditioned being you come to the unfathomable, if you deny the life of things and of conditioned being you stand before nothingness, if you hallow this life you meet the living God."

Zen Scholars and Buber

In my dialogue with Suzuki, Nishitani, Chang Chi-Chen, and a number of Western Zen scholars, I have not found important divergence from this similarity between Buber and Zen. On the other hand, in an intensive dialogue lasting for a number of months with my former colleague Richard DeMartino, whose term "nondual dualism" expresses just what I have been trying to say, there has been such divergence. This is because DeMartino insists on seeing Buber's "I-Thou" philosophy as a dualism essentially similar to the subject-object dualism which it is held to overcome. It is also because, in contrast to Buber who holds that the I-Thou relationship comes first in the life of the child and only then the I-It, DeMartino holds that the

I-It relationship is the basic experience, a sort of "fall" which can only be overcome by getting through the "Great Doubt Block." Into his existential interpretation of Zen, DeMartino imports concepts of Reinhold Niebuhr's and Sartre's that sharpen unduly the differences between Buber and Zen.

Basically this is a question of philosophical anthropology, how one understands man as such. There is also a difference, to be sure, between the Rinzai understanding of *satori* as sudden enlightenment and Buber's gradual bringing of the world of It into the world of Thou in which the swinging between the two poles is a necessary part of this redemptive movement. In this Buber is perhaps more akin to the Taoist sense of the swinging opposites of yin and yang than to Zen. Yet the Soto sect of Zen and even many scholars of the Rinzai sect deny that *satori* is a once-for-all matter, however much the experience of enlightenment itself may appear to be a decisive breakthrough.

What we can conclude is that, while largely overlooked except by such Zen scholars as Nishitani and Hisamatsu, Buber's dialogue with Oriental religions, and with Taoism and Zen in particular, is of great importance, second only to his dialogue with Christianity. This can be brought out through one last illustration—Buber's interpretation of the Hasidic concept of *kavana,* or intention, its affinity with the philosophies of action implicit in Hinduism, Taoism, and Zen Buddhism, and the social ethic that grows out of these related approaches to action.

The Meaning of *Kavana*

In "The Life of the Hasidim," the introductory section of *The Legend of the Baal-Shem,* Buber describes *kavana* as a whole-hearted service of God that does not mean turning away from one's fellows or from the world. All that is asked is to do everything one does with one's whole strength—not the denial of self and the extirpation of the passions but the fulfillment of self and the direction of passion in a communal mysticism of humility, love, prayer, and joy. Fulfillment and redemption do "not take place through formulae or through any kind of prescribed and special action," but through the *kavana* that one brings to one's every act. "It is not the matter of the action, but only its dedication that is decisive." In Hasidism, as Buber interprets it, it is not the doctrine that is important but the way of life, the image of the human. Words are of importance when they manifest life, not when they take its place. The Baal Shem once refused to enter a synagogue because it was crowded form floor to ceiling and wall to wall with prayers that had been uttered without real devotion. Even the right mood is of no avail if the motivation is wrong: the man who prays in sorrow because of the bleakness which burdens his spirit does not know the real fear of God, and the man who prays in joy because of the radiance of his spirit does not know the love of God. His "fear is the burden of sadness, and his love is nothing but empty joy." Honest grief, in contrast, is that of a man who knows what he lacks, while the truly joyful man is like someone whose house has burned down and who begins to build anew out of the deep need of his soul: "Over every stone that is laid, his heart rejoices."

Once the Maggid of Mezritch let a sigh escape when, as a young man, he was poor and his baby was too weak even to cry. Instantly a voice said: "You have lost your share in the world to come." "Good," exclaimed the Maggid. "Now I can begin to serve in good earnest!" *Kavana* does not mean that what is important is "purity of heart" but that one must bring oneself with all one's possibility of response into every action. This is the Hasidic image of the human: "Only he who brings himself to the Lord as an offering may be called man." This bringing of oneself is no once-for-all commitment but an ever-renewed finding of direction, a responding to the call in each new hour. The Hasidic demand that we discover and perform our own created task, that we channel the passion of the "evil" urge into the realization of our personal uniqueness, that we act and love with *kavana,* or inner intention, implies the strongest possible rejection of all those ways whereby we divide our lives into airtight compartments and escape becoming whole. Becoming whole does not mean "spiritual" wholeness or the wholeness of the individuated Self within the unconscious (to use the language of Jung). It means that personal wholeness, the necessary corollary of which is the wholeness of our lives. When one disciple of Rabbi Bunam asked another, "To what purpose was man created?" the latter replied, "So that he might perfect his soul." "No, indeed," said the former. "He was created so that he might lift up the heavens!" Our true wholeness is not the perfection of our "immortal soul" but the fulfillment of our created task. Only the latter brings our personal uniqueness into being in integral relation with the creation over against which we are set. To make our goal spiritual perfection, consequently, means a foreshortening of our personal existence.

To Be Humanly Holy

The rabbi of Kotzk explained the biblical injunction, "Ye shall be holy unto me," as the demand not for perfection but for authentic humanity: "You shall be holy unto me, but as men. You shall be humanly holy unto me." We are not asked to be superhuman saints but to be holy in the measure and manner of the human, in the measure and manner of our personal resources. This is a seemingly easier demand than perfection, but, in fact, it is harder; for it asks you to do what you really can do rather than despair over what you cannot. We take our ideas and ideals with grim seriousness, says Martin Buber, but we do not allow them to have a binding claim upon our everyday lives. "No amount of hypocritical piety has ever reached this concentrated degree of inauthenticity!" Our wretchedness is due to the fact that we do not open our lives to the holy, Buber adds and then concludes: "A life that is not open to the holy is not only unworthy of spirit, it is unworthy of life." This is not a question of being punished for being "unworthy." It is a matter of the meaning of life itself.

To open our lives to the holy does not mean to rise above our situation. It means to bring our situation into dialogue with God. The openness to the holy does not mean leaving the everyday for a higher spiritual sphere but "hallowing the everyday" through a genuine openness to what meets you. "Whoever says that the words of the Torah are one thing and the words of the world another," said Rabbi Pinhas of Koretz, "must be regarded as a man who denies God." The rabbi of Rizhyn imposed upon a confirmed sinner a terrible penance: "From now until you die, you shall not utter a single word of prayer with empty lips; but you shall preserve the fulness of every word." The sinner himself had brought the rabbi the long list of his sins to have penance imposed upon him. The rabbi's response not only demanded a sincere inner repentance but a wholehearted turning of his existence. Only thus could a man who was used to living moment by moment in inner division bring the whole of his intention and the whole of his life into prayer. "What does it amount to that they expound the Torah!" cried Rabbi Leib, son of Sara. "A man should see to it that all his actions are a Torah and that he himself becomes so entirely a Torah that one can learn from his habits and his motions and his motionless clinging to God." The rabbi of Kobryn taught:

God says to man, as he said to Moses: "Put off thy shoes from thy feet"—put off the habitual which encloses your foot, and you will know that the place on which you are now standing is holy ground. For there is no rung of human life on which we cannot find the holiness of God everywhere and at all times.[14]

The true opposite of "the habitual" is not the extraordinary or the unusal but the fresh, the open, the ever-new of the person who recognizes the unique situation in which he or she stands as the ground of hallowing and hallows the everyday.

The Way to Do Is to Be

"He who knows the action that is in inaction, the inaction that is in action is wise indeed," says the Bhagavad-gītā. "The way to do is to be," says Lao-tzu. Gandhi's satyāgraha, truth-force or nonviolent direct action; the Buddha's refusal to give or accept injury; Lao-tzu's *wu wei,* the action of the whole being that flows with the Tao and does not interfere; the importance of *kavana,* or inner intention, of Hasidism—if there is one thing that is in common to all of these, it is a philosophy of action that makes doing integral with being and rejects any ethic that is less than a claim on the whole person. This also means that we ought not to deny or neglect action for the sake of inwardness. We cannot achieve wholeness by going inward and leaving the outward secondary and inessential, anymore than we can achieve it by going outward and neglecting the inward. If we have such a split between inner and outer, then our so-called "inner, essential self" is going to atrophy, and it will not be a real person at all.

The Buddha's refusal to deal with metaphysical matters—with "questions that tend not to edification"—focuses us in on what we are doing in the here and now. Zen, too, stresses that real action and real being have to do with "this moment," the now, with where we are now and what we are doing now. The most important thing to Hasidism is whatever one happens to be doing at the moment; for *kavana* means being present in the present, being a presence to others and allowing them to be present to oneself. The center of Taoism, similarly, is "The way to do is to be." This statement is entirely misinterpreted if one thinks it means turning inward and away from the beings with whom one lives. Lao-tzu, in contrast, teaches an oscillating interaction between inner and outer, for the Tao is not located in any particular place. "You do not need a window for better seeing," says Lao-tzu. "Rather abide at the center of your being." But the Tao is never found except through opening one's center to one's fellow beings and the world: "A sound man's heart is not shut within itself."

If there ought be no dualism of "sacred" words and "secular" words, neither ought there be a dualism between words and silence. When the Yehudi discovered that a young man had taken a vow of silence for 3 years except for the Torah and prayer, he called the young man to him and asked him why it was that he did not see a single word of his in the world of truth. When the young man justified his silence by talking of the "vanity of speech," the Yehudi warned him that he who only learns and prays is murdering the world of his own soul. "What do you mean by the 'vanity of speech'?"asked the Yehudi. "Whatever you have to say can be vanity or it can be truth." In contrast to the currently popular dualism between "words" and "feelings," Lao-tzu, like the Yehudi, says, "Real words are not vain and vain words are not real." A *real* word embodies the movement of the Tao between being and being. A *vain* word prevents this movement of the Tao. It shuts the Tao out and hides itself away; for it will not risk itself, it will not give itself. The way of Taoism, like the way of

Zen Buddhism and of Hasidism, is *inner* and *outer* both, and it is *between*. "He who is anciently aware of existence is master of each moment," says Lao-tzu. I do not have to split my existence into a phenomenal "unreal" present as opposed to a "real" but not present essence somewhere transcending it. I can take each moment as it comes. "What more do I need to know of origin than this?"

8

Religious Education as Dialogue

In the "Gleanings" that, just before his death, Buber selected from his miscellaneous writings for preservation and publication, there is one short paragraph on "religious education:"

> If faith signifies not a mere conviction or certainty that something is, but a binding oneself to something, an involvement of one's own person, an immeasurably binding venture, then there is no education for faith. But there is an education to this insight as to what faith is and what it is not. One can lead no one to real faith, but one can show another the face of real faith, show it so clearly that he will not henceforth confuse faith with its artful ape, "religious" feeling. And one can teach him *with what* one believes when one really believes: with the lived moment and ever again with the lived moment. But if anywhere, this education begins in the realm of the deepest self-recollection: there where one questions himself, decides, and puts himself to the test.[1]

As I type these words that I myself translated a dozen years ago, they bring to my mind the way of teaching of

Shneur Zalman of Ladi, "The Rav" of Northern White Russia and the founder of the Habad, or Lubavitcher, Hasidism to which my grandfather and great-grandfather belonged. The rav asked a disciple who had just entered his room: "Moshe, what do we mean when we say 'God'?" The disciple was silent. The rav asked him a second and third time and then asked him why he was silent. "Because I do not know," replied the disciple. "Do you think I know?" exclaimed the rav. "But I must say it, for it is so, and therefore I must say it: He is definitely there, and except for him nothing is definitely there—and this is He." This, if anything, is religious education as dialogue, as dialogical existentialism. The rav does not point to general propositions of faith nor does he claim any abstract knowledge of God that would enable him to define or describe him. What he points to, instead, is just the most concrete, particular, and unique, what the Zen Buddhist would call "suchness," and this very particular "is He."

When the rav once asked his son with what he prayed, he was even more concrete and particular. The son, thinking his father meant what scriptual passage did he base his prayer on, answered: "With the verse: 'Every stature shall prostrate itself before thee.' " But when the son asked his father, "With what do you pray?", the latter answered, "With the floor and with the bench." He did not mean that they supported his body while he prayed, but that he literally prayed with them. Once when a Hasid started to pray in one place and then changed his mind and went to another, the first place called out: "What is wrong with me that you do not pray over me? And if I am bad, is it not for you to redeem me?"!

True Religious Communication

Once Martin Buber gave a series of speeches to an audience in which there were a number of workers. But he became increasingly troubled by the fact that none of them spoke up. At the end of his third lecture, a young worker came up to him and said, "You know, we cannot speak here. But if you would meet with us alone tomorrow, we could talk with you." Buber agreed and on the next day, a Sunday, he had a full and free discussion with the workers alone. During the course of the discussion, he was confronted by a man who said slowly and impressively, in the words the astronomer LaPlace is said to have used to Napoleon, "I do not need this hypothesis 'God' in order to be at home in the world." Feeling himself more severely challenged than by the others, Buber countered by shaking up the security of the naturalistic world-view of this worker, whom he imagined had been influenced by the lectures of a noted natural scientist of that industrial city. We cannot understand either the objects that we see, nor ourselves that see them, nor our evanescent but nonetheless real meleting with them, Buber pointed out, drawing on a twentieth-century physics more sophisticated than any the worker had access to. Where then is the world and its security? "What is this being that gives this 'world,' which has become so questionable, its foundation?"

When Buber was through speaking, the worker, who had kept his eyes lowered the whole time, raised his eyes and said, equally slowly and impressively, "You are right." Buber sat in front of him dismayed. He had led him, he realized, to what Pascal called the "God of the Philosophers" and not to the God of Abraham, Isaac, and Jacob—the Living God to whom one can say "Thou." Despite his seeming success in getting the worker to accept "God," Buber concludes this report of a venture in "religious education" on a note of failure:

> On the next day I had to depart. I could not remain, as I now ought to do; I could not enter into the factory where the man worked, become his comrade, live with him, win his trust through real life-relationship, help him to walk with me the

way of the creature who *accepts* the creation. I could only return his gaze.[2]

Religious education must itself be "dialogue" or it is neither religion nor education. And dialogue is not intellectual dialectic but the real meeting and full personal interchange in the course of lived life between two persons each of whom allows the other to exist as an independent "other" and not just as a content of his own experience or an object to be placed in his mental categories. From this point of view, communication of trust, of responsiveness, of one's real relation to being is more important than agreement on matters of creed. But this communication, to be genuine, must be more than expression of objective ideas or of subjective feelings. It must be a real listening and responding in which the unspoken dialogue is as important as the spoken.

Once in conversation with a great German thinker, Buber was called on to defend himself for using the word God. "What you mean by the word," said his opponent, "is something beyond all human grasp and comprehension, but in speaking of it you have degraded it and have brought in its train all the innocent blood, injustice, misuse, and blasphemy which have defiled and desecrated it through countless centuries." "Just for this reason I may not abandon it," Buber replied.

Generations of men have laid the burden of their anxious lives upon it. Men murder one another and say "In God's name;" but when all madness and delusion fall to dust, when they stand over against Him in the loneliest darkness and no longer say, "He, He" but rather sigh "Thou," and add "God," is it not the real God whom they all implore, the one Living God? . . . We cannot cleanse the word "God" and we cannot make it whole; but, defiled and mutilated as it is, we can raise it from the ground and set it over an hour of great care."

In this case, the interchange did not end in agreement, as in Buber's discussion with the worker, but here were true dialogue and true religious communication such as were not present in the other encounter. And it is thus that Buber reported it:

> The old man stood up, came over to me, laid his hand on my shoulder, and spoke: "Let us be friends." The conversation was completed. For where two or three are truly together, they are together in the name of God."[3]

The Religious Symbol and the Lived Event

The highest manifestation of the religious symbol is a human life lived in relation to the Absolute. One of the most effective methods of religious education, in consequence, as all religious educators know, is the image of the person whose life makes manifest her or his meeting with God—whether the saint, the seer, the prophet, or the humble person of faith. This is not the image of the person in abstraction from situation, but in the heart of the lived event. The true symbol derives from and points back to the relation between person and person, person and situation, person and nature, person and art. The symbol does not hover timelessly over concrete actualities. "Whenever the symbol appears, it owes its appearance always to the unforeseen, unique occasion," writes Buber, "to its having appeared the first time."

The Task of the Modern Educator

The religious educator may not legitimately impose religious beliefs and values on her charges. What she does communicate must take place in a dialogical relationship founded on respect for the created uniqueness of each of her students. On the other hand, neither is she called to a permissiveness or simple good-fellowship that turns her task of religious education into a sharing on the part of equals. To act as teacher or pastor one must avoid both the pitfalls of the sermonizer and of the discussion moderator. Buber once described the "old" and the "new" educators by the figures of the "funnel" and the "pump." The "funnel" educators emphasize "objective" education, which they picture as the passive reception of tradition poured in from above. The "pump" educators emphasize the "subjective" and picture education as drawing forth the powers of the self. To these objective and subjective approaches—which Buber describes in another essay by still another set of figures, those of the "sculpture" and the "gardener"—Buber's dialogical philosophy of education offers a genuine and highly significant third alternative. In the pupil's meeting with the person of the teacher and the "Thou" of the writer, the reality which they present to her is transformed from the potential, abstract, and unrelated to the actual, concrete, and present immediacy of a person and even, in a sense, a reciprocal relationship.[4]

Extending Buber's distinction to the field of religious education, we might be tempted to characterize the objective approach to religious education as the "catechetical" and the subjective as the "inspirational." Oversimplified as this distinction is, it is suggestive of some of the underlying trends that do exist today and that correspond to such deep religious divergences as those between the "orthodox," fundamentalist, or "neo-Orthodox" approaches, on the one hand, and the various "liberal" approaches on the other.

The modern religious educator is confronted by two all-pervasive problems that threaten his enterprise at its very heart. The first is what Buber speaks of as the tendency of modern man to establish a dualism between life in the spirit and life in the world. The second is what Buber calls the "eclipse of God." Both are aspects of one basic attitude of modern man: his desire to free his everyday existence from any inconvenient claim upon him to hallow his life by making it responsible to what is holy. This desire he fulfills equally well by removing his relation with God into a "pure" world of the spirit, by denying that relation, or by subjectivizing it so that it becomes purely immanent—identical with man's inspirations and aspirations. The special problem for the modern religious educator is not so much the straightforward atheist who denies God and who may, indeed, be prompted by an essentially religious integrity. It is the person who accepts religion but spiritualizes or subjectivizes it, negating it at its core by denying its claim on his life.

"It is the signature of our time that the spirit imposes no obligations," writes Buber.

Everything except everyday life belongs to the realm of the spirit. . . . Nowadays "religion" itself is part of the detached spirit. It is one of the subdivisions—which is in high favor, to be sure—of the structure erected over and above life, one of the rooms on the top floor, with a very special atmosphere of its own.

If the contemporary person "takes any interest" at all in the Scriptures, correspondingly, it is an abstract, purely "religious" interest.

More often not even that, but an interest connected with the history of religion or civilization, or an aesthetic interest. . . . He no longer confronts his life with the Word; he locks life away in one of many unholy compartments. . . . Man of today resists the Scriptures because he cannot endure revelation. To endure revelation is to endure this moment full of possible decisions, to respond to and be responsible for every moment. Man of today resists the Scriptures because he does not want any longer to accept responsibility.[5]

"Either the teachings live in the life of a responsible human being or they are not alive at all." This is not a question of a humanly unattainable completeness and perfection but of the willingness to do what we can at every instant, the willingness to answer for our whole life.

The men in the Bible are sinners like ourselves, but there is one sin they do not commit, our arch-sin: they do not dare confine God to a circumscribed space or division of life, to "religion," . . . they do not presume to draw boundaries around God's commandments and say to him: "Up to this point, you are sovereign, but beyond these bounds begins the sovereignty of science or society or the state."[6]

In our age, writes Buber, which knows no figure of general validity, such as the Christian, the gentleman, or the citizen was for other ages, the image of the imageless God "is the indefinable, only factual, direction of the responsible modern educator." The modern educator is set in the *imitatio Dei absconditi sed non ignoti.*"[7] But to typically modern man the "hiding God" is the "dead God." The real meaning of the "death of God," of which Nietzsche, Heidegger, and Sartre speak, says Buber, is "that man has become incapable of apprehending a reality absolutely independent of himself and of having a relation with it." "Eclipse of the light of heaven, eclipse of God" is, as Buber sees it, "the character of the historical hour through which the world is passing." Idealism and the various types of modern relativism that have succeeded it—immanentism, psychologism, evolutionism, historicism, naturalism, materialism—have all contributed to dissolving "all partnership of existence" in "free-floating subjectivity." What is in question in this process is not just atheism. The traditional term "God" is preserved in many cases "for the sake of its profound overtones, but in such a way that any connection it may have with our concrete life as a life exposed to the manifestations of God, must become meaningless." "Specifically modern thought can no longer endure a God who is not confined to man's subjectivity, who is not merely a 'supreme value.' " It seeks to preserve the idea of the divine as the true concern of religion and at the same time to destroy the reality of our relation to him. "This is done in many ways," writes Buber, "overtly and covertly, apodictically and hypothethically, in the language of metaphysics and of psychology."[8]

In modern philosophy of religion the I of the I-It relation steps ever more into the foreground as the "subject" of "religious feeling," the "profiter from a pragmatist decision to believe." Perhaps the greatest single danger for the modern religious educator is the widespread tendency to make religion "accessible" by appealing to the "pragmatic"—what religion offers by way of "peace of mind" and "peace of soul," "self-realization" and enriched experience, success, and harmonious community living. At the point where these become the goals rather than the by-products, then the product is not religion but the latest form of idolatry. Along with pragmatism goes that inspirationalism and the subjectivizing of the act of faith itself which have penetrated to the innermost depth of modern religious life. This subjectivization threatens the spontaneous turning toward the Presence with which the person who prays formerly overcame what distracted his or her attention. "The over consciousness of this man here that he is praying, that he is *praying,* that *he* is praying . . . depossesses the moment, takes away its spontaneity." His subjectivity enters into the midst of his statement of trust and disturbs his relation with the Absolute.[9]

Our link with God is the beginning, writes Buber, "and

the function of the teachings is to make us aware of our bond and make it fruitful." Tradition must include at once continuity and spontaneity, transmission and begetting. "The teachings themselves are the way." The continuity of Judaism, for example, "does not imply the preservation of the old, but the ceaseless begetting and giving birth to the same single spirit, and its continuous integration into life." "Only the teachings truly rejuvenated can liberate us from limitations and bind us to the unconditional." The merely social, merely national, merely religious lack the fiery breath of the teachings which rekindles the spark of revelation.[10] But neither can this spark be rekindled through the fictitious approach to tradition which exalts its works and values as the subject of pride and piety, teaching the tradition "but not with the purpose of seriously integrating it into actual life." Buber describes as "wholly unfruitful," however, the attempt to revive religious forms without their religious content—an attempt that characterizes significant segments of the "religious revival" in the contemporary world.

Forms themselves are nothing. What value they have accrues to them only through what has been expressed in them, what has pervaded them as the soul pervades the body. The secret of their origin is the secret of their effectiveness. Once they have grown empty, one cannot fill them with a new, timely content; they will not hold it. Once they have decayed, they cannot be resuscitated by infusion with a spirit other than their own. They will seem as lifelike as dolls. All such attempts are dilettantish—devoid of reverence and vigor; they are unblessed. A Passover Seder which is held to celebrate the national liberation as such will always be lacking in the essential, and that essential can only be won when we feel that self-liberation only enfolds the redemption of man and the world through a redeeming power as the husk enfolds the kernel.[11]

The basic problem that Buber confronts here is not that of the Jewish tradition alone but of all modern religion: "What shall we do when a generation, like that of today, has become alienated from the religious content of the forms?" Here it is the task of the religious educator to help her students surmount the prejudice of the era that treats the Scriptures only as literary, cultural, or religious history and to help them surmount "the superstition of the era" which holds "that the world of faith to which those utterances bear witness is the subject of our knowledge only and not a reality which makes life worth living."

> This generation must be made receptive . . . to the voice of the mystery which speaks in those utterances. And we should not do all this with the purpose of preparing them to repeat the teachings and perform prescribed rites, but so that they may acquire the power to make the original choice, that—listening to the voice with that power—they may hear the message it has for their hour and their work; that they may learn to trust the voice, and through this trust, come to faith, to a faith of their own.[12]

The great Hasidic rebbe Levi Yitzhak of Berditchev identified himself with that fourth son in the Passover Haggadah who is so young that he does not know how to ask why this night is different from all other nights. But he did know how to ask what the meaning and message of the present moment of history was for him, what God was asking him, and the people of Israel, and all mankind by way of it:

> I do not know how to ask you, Lord of the world, and even if I did know, I could not bear to do it. How could I venture to ask you why everything happens as it does, why we are driven from one exile into another, why our foes are allowed to torment us so?

The Haggadah says that the father must ask for this youngest son, and to Levi Yitzhak it was precisely the Lord of the world who was his father and who should ask for him. But he wanted no gnosis, no revelation of secret mysteries, only the heart of the life of dialogue—the pointing to what he might do and how he might live:

> I do not beg you to reveal to me the secret of your ways—I could not bear it! But show me one thing; show it to me more clearly and more deeply: show me what this, which is happening at this very moment, means to me, what it demands of me, what you, Lord of the world, are telling me by way of it. Ah, it is not why I suffer that I wish to know, but only whether I suffer for your sake.[13]

9

Existential Trust and the Eclipse of God

*I*n 1975, on the tenth anniversary of Martin Buber's death, I spoke at a conference in Washington, D.C., on "The Continuing Buber." For me, the "Continuing Buber" is really our continuing dialogue with Buber who remains present with us addressing, challenging and comforting. Like the story of the Baal Shem Tov who spoke to a group in such a way that each person felt he was speaking to him, Martin Buber speaks to the condition of many, many people, even though many of these people cannot speak with one another.

Mystical Inwardness and the Life of Dialogue

Martin Buber is like the man in the Hasidic tale who made the long journey to Prague on foot becuase he had dreamed three times of a treasure hidden under a bridge there, only to discover from the captain of the guard that the treasure was hidden beneath his own stove in Krakow. He would not have found authentic existence "here where one stands" if he had not first made the journey to

"Prague." He would not have reached that "basic trust" which was central to his life ever since if he had not gone through the mystical, but also he would not have reached it had he simply remained in the mystical. After he had given up the metaphysical structure which claims that the mystic becomes one with the All, he still retained the residue of immediacy and presentness necessary for understanding the "I-Thou" relationship.

One of the most important double pulls experienced by modern man is that between the exploration of "inner space" through mystic meditation and the call to make real the space *between* person and person in the life of dialogue. This is not a question of "inner" versus "outer," since the interhuman, when it is genuine, demands that the inwardness and uniqueness of each partner be brought into the meeting. In his "conversion" from mystic ecstasy to the world, Buber wished to bring the mystic inwardness he had known into the full reality of the present—to make it present in his response. He no longer made it an end in itself. What Buber said in his contrast between gnosis and *devotio* we could say of his own life path: "Where the mystic vortex circled now stretches the way of man."

Asked in *Philosophical Interrogations* what he would regard as the central portion of his lifework, Buber responded that it was not anything individual but only the one basic insight that led him to the study of the Bible and Hasidism but also to his independent philosophy: "that the I-Thou relation to God and the I-Thou relation to one's fellow man are at bottom related to each other. . . . All my work on the Bible has ultimately served this insight."[1]

In a Time of God's Hiddenness

Buber's faith was based upon his experiences of faith, including that threat of infinity that brought him close to suicide as a boy of fourteen and the "eclipse of God" which haunted him during the post-Holocaust years. In *Between Man and Man* Buber stated that the present epoch of "homelessness" has proceeded out of the Copernican invasion of the infinite. But in *Philosophical Interrogations* he added that "this invasion has had the effect that it had only because man has merely opposed to it the Kantian antinomy of the infinity and finiteness of space and time." So far we have not opposed to this invasion "a greater image of God than the traiditonal one, a greater one *and yet one that can still be addressed,* the image of a God who out of his eternity has set in being this infinite-finite, space-time world, who embraces and rules over it with his eternity." The awful silence of the spaces between the stars that terrified Pascal and the "indefiniteness that shadows forth the heartless voids and immensities of the universe and stabs us from behind with the thought of annihilation" (Melville), Buber enclosed with a renewed and deepened existential trust.

This existential trust was in no way incompatible with that "eclipse of God" to which Buber pointed again and again during the last years of his life. The silence of the transcendence combined with the perseverance of the religious need in modern man may have an entirely different meaning than Sartre imagined, Buber suggested in *Eclipse of God.* If God is silent toward man and man toward God, "then something has taken place, not in human subjectivity but in Being itself. It would be worthier not to explain it to oneself in sensational and incompetent sayings, such as that of the 'death' of God, but to endure it as it is and at the same time to move existentially toward a new happening, toward that event in which the word between heaven and earth will again be heard." Buber later expanded this thought in a statement on my book *Problematic Rebel,* a statement that shows with utmost clarity that his opposition to Sartre could not be attributed to any romantic optimism:

> The theme of *Problematic Rebel* is the revolt of man against an existence emptied of meaning, the existence after the so-called "death of God." This emptying of meaning is not to be overcome through the illusionary program of a free "creation of values," as we know it in Nietzsche and Sartre. One must withstand this meaninglessness, must suffer it to the end, must do battle with it undauntedly, until out of the contradiction experienced in conflict and suffering, meaning shines forth anew.

It was the Holocaust above all that manifested the "eclipse of God" for Buber with a horror that assaulted existential trust in a way that neither Pascal nor Melville could have imagined. Buber confessed that there was not an hour when he did not think of it. "When God seems to withdraw himself utterly from the earth and no longer participates in its existence," Buber wrote in "The Dialogue between Heaven and Earth," "the space of history is full of noise but empty of the divine breath." Buber stated that one who believes in the living God, who knows about Him, and is fated to spend his life in a time of his hiddenness, finds it very difficult to live. This is an unmistakably personal confession. Buber ended this essay with the question of how a life with God is still possible in a time in which there is an Auschwitz. In a chapter in my *Hidden Human Image*, "Elie Wiesel: the Job of Auschwitz," I quote Wiesel, himself a survivor of the Holocaust, as saying that "with the advent of the Nazi regime . . . humanity became witness to what Martin Buber would call an eclipse of God." It was above all, in fact, in the name of the "Job of Auschwitz" that Buber called this an age of the "eclipse of God."

"The estrangement has become too cruel, the hiddenness too deep,'' Buber wrote. Can we still speak to God, hear this word, call to him, or, as an individual or as a people, enter into dialogue with him? ''Dare we recommend to the survivors of Auschwitz, the Job of the gas chambers: 'Give thanks unto the Lord, for He is good; for His mercy endureth forever'?'' The only answer that Job receives is God's nearness, that he knows God again. ''Nothing is explained, nothing adjusted; wrong has not become right, nor cruelty kindness.'' And how is it with us, Buber asked, with ''all those who have not got over what happened and will not get over it?'' Buber answered this question with the trust and contending of the ''Modern Job'':

> Do we stand overcome before the hidden face of God like the tragic hero of the Greeks before faceless fate? No, rather even now we contend, we too, with God, even with Him, the Lord of Being, whom we once, we here, chose for our Lord. We do not put up with earthly being; we struggle for its redemption, and struggling we appeal to the help of our Lord, who is again and still a hiding one . . . Though His coming appearance resemble no earlier one, we shall recognize again our cruel and merciful Lord.[2]

''We experience this not only as an hour of the heaviest affliction,'' Buber wrote in 1952, ''but also as one that appears to give no essentially different outlook for the future, no prospect of a time of radiant and full living.'' With each new crisis in man's image of the universe ''the original contract between the universe and man is dissolved and man finds himself a stranger and solitary in the world.'' As a result of this insecurity, man questions not only the universe and his relation to it, but himself. Today, writes Buber, ''the question about man's being faces us as never before in all its grandeur and terror—no longer in philosophical attire but in the nakedness of existence.'' In other eras of cosmic insecurity there was still "a *social* certainty" resulting from "living in real togetherness" in "a small organic community." Modern man, in contrast, is homeless both in the universe and in the community. Our modern crisis, as a result, is the most deep-reaching and comprehensive in history. In it the two aspects of social and cosmic insecurity have merged into a loss of confidence in human existence as such:

> The existential mistrust is indeed basically no longer, like the old kind, a mistrust of my fellow-man. It is rather the destruction of confidence in existence in general. That we can no longer carry on a genuine conversation from one camp to the other is the severest symtpom of the sickness of present-day man. Existential mistrust is this sickness itself. But the destruction of trust in human existence is the inner poisoning of the total human organism from which this sickness stems.[3]

The Loss of Trust in God

The loss of confidence in human existence also means a loss of trust in God. "At its core the conflict between mistrust and trust of man conceals the conflict between mistrust and trust of eternity." In the way leading from one age of solitude to the next, "each solitude is colder and stricter than the preceding, and salvation from it more difficult." It is only in our time, however, that man has reached a condition in which "he can no longer stretch his hands out from his solitude to meet a divine form." This inability to reach out to God is at the basis of Nietzsche's saying, "God is dead." "Apparently nothing more remains now to the solitary man but to seek an intimate communication with himself." Modern man is imprisoned in his subjectivity and cannot discern "the essential difference between all subjectivity and that which transcends it."

In the progress of its philosophizing the human spirit is

ever more inclined to regard the absolute which it contemplates as having been produced by itself, the spirit that thinks it: "Until, finally, all that is over against us, everything that accosts us and takes possession of us, all partnership of existence, is dissolved in free-floating subjectivity." In the next age, which is the modern one, the human spirit annihilates conceptually the absoluteness of the absolute. Although the spirit may imagine that it still remains "as bearer of all things and coiner of all values," it has annihilated its own absoluteness as well. "Spirit" is now only a product of human individuals "which they contain and secrete like mucus and urine."

Gnosis and Jung

Even more eloquent than Nietzsche's proclamation that God is dead, writes Buber, are the attempts to fill the now-empty horizon. One of these is that gnosis which attempts to see through the contradiction of existence and free itself from it, rather than endure the contradiction and redeem it. This gnosis is not found in the modern world in theosophies and occult systems alone. "In many theologies also, unveiling gestures are to be discovered behind the interpreting ones." Gnosis has even found its way into modern psychotherapy through the teachings of Carl Jung, as Buber has shown at length in the sections of *Eclipse of God* devoted to Jung. In Jung's teaching the integrated soul "dispenses with the conscience as the court which distinguishes and decides between right and wrong." The precondition for this integration is the " 'liberation from those desires, ambitions, and passions which imprison us in the visible world.' " through " 'intelligent fulfilment of instinctive demands.' " What this means becomes clear through Jung's statement that it is necessary to succumb, "in part", to evil in order that the unification of good and evil may

take place. Jung thus resumes, under the guise of psychotherapy, the gnostic motif "of mystically deifying the instincts."

> The psychological doctrine which deal with mysteries without
> knowing the attitude of faith toward mystery is the modern
> manifestation of gnosis. Gnosis is not to be understood as only
> a historical category, but as a universal one. It—and not athe-
> ism, which annihilates God because it must reject the hitherto
> existing images of God—is the real antagonist of the reality of
> faith.[4]

Jung conceives of God as an "autonomous psychic content," "a function of the unconscious," writes Buber.
What the believer ascribes to God has its origin in his own
soul; for Jung's God cannot exist independently of man.

> Man does not deny a transcendent God; he simply dispenses
> with Him. He no longer knows the Unrecognizable; he no
> longer needs to pretend to know Him. In His place he knows
> the soul or rather the self. . . . Whatever may be the case
> concerning God, the important thing for the man of modern
> consciousness is to stand in no further relation of faith to
> Him.[5]

The self, the bridal unification of good and evil, is elevated
by Jung into the new "Incarnation," and the idea of God
is replaced by that of the deified or divine man. Jung's
psychology of religion is to be understood as the announcement of the gnostic god who embraces Christ and
Satan, God and man, as the Coming One.

Heidegger and the Historic Hour

Martin Heidegger is more explicit than Jung in his announcement of "the Coming One." Heidegger intimates

that after our present imageless era—the era in which "God is dead"—a new procession of divine images may begin. But he does not hold, says Buber, that man will again experience and accept his real encounters with the divine as such. What brings about the reappearance of the divine, in Heidegger's view, is human thought about truth; for Being, to Heidegger, attains its illumination through the destiny and history of man. "He whose appearance can be effected or co-effected through such a modern-magical influence," writes Buber, "clearly has only the name in common with Him whom we men, basically in agreement despite all the differences in our religious teachings, address as God." Heidegger ends, Buber points out, by allying to his own historical hour this clarification of the thought of being to which he has ascribed the power to make ready for the sunrise of the holy. "History exists," writes Heidegger, "only when the essence of truth is originally decided." Yet the hour that he has affirmed as history in this sense is none other than that of Hitler and the Nazis, "the very same hour whose problematics in its most inhuman manifestation led him astray." When Heidegger proclaims Hitler as "the present and future German reality and its law," writes Buber, "history no longer stands, as in all believing times, under divine judgment, but it itself, the unappealable, assigns to the Coming One his way."[6]

Heidegger was able to make a mistake of such dimensions because, like Hegel, he glimpsed no eternity that might be set over against time as a transcendent reality that limits and judges it. Even though Heidegger appears to attain a type of absolute through his doctrine of the disclosure of Being through man in history, this is not a doctrine that admits "man's boldest concept, that of eternity set in judgment above the whole course of history and thereby above each historical age." Instead historical time and history are absolutized, as a result of which Hitler's drive to power is also absolutized, and "the goblin called success, convulsively grinning," occupies "for a while the divine seat of authority."

> Time is not embraced by the timeless, and the ages do not shudder before One who does not dwell in time but only appears in it. The knowledge has vanished that time can in no wise be conceived as a finally existing reality, independent and self-contained, and that absurdity lies in wait for every attempt to reflect on it in this way no matter whether time be contemplated as finite or as infinite.[7]

The Human Responsibility for the Eclipse

When he has to interpret his encounters with God as self-encounters, "man's very structure is destroyed," writes Buber. "This is the portent of the present hour."

> In our age the I-It relation, gigantically swollen, has usurped, practically uncontested, the mastery and the rule. The I of this relation, an I that possesses all, makes all, succeeds with all, this I that is unable to say Thou, unable to meet a being essentially, is the lord of the hour. This selfhood that has become omnipotent, with all the It around it, can naturally acknowledge neither God nor any genuine absolute which manifests itself to men as of non-human origin. It steps in between and shuts off from us the light of heaven.[8]

"He who refuses to submit himself to the effective reality of the transcendence," writes Buber, ". . . contributes to the human responsibility for the eclipse." This does not mean that man can effect "the death of God." Even if there is no longer "a God of man," He who is denoted by the name "lives intact" in the light of His eternity. "But we, 'the slayers,' remain dwellers in darkness, consigned to death." Thus the real meaning of the proclamation that God is "dead" is "that man has become incapable of apprehending a reality absolutely independent of himself and of having a relation with it." Heidegger is right in saying that we can no longer image God, but this is not a lack in man's imagination. "The great images of God . . . are born not of imagination but of real encounters with real divine power and glory." Man's power to glimpse God with his being's eye yields no images since God eludes direct contemplation, but it is from this glimpse that all images and representations are born.

When the I of the I-It relation comes in between man and God, that glance through which man glimpsed God with his being's eye is no longer possible, and, as a result, the image-making power of the human heart declines. "Man's capacity to apprehend the divine in images is lamed in the same measure as is his capacity to experience a reality absolutely independent of himself." In all past times men had, stored away in their hearts, images of the Absolute, "partly pallid, partly crude, altogether false and yet true. . . ." These images helped to protect them from the deception of the voices, the apes of God. This protection no longer exists now that "God is dead," now that the "spiritual pupil" cannot catch a glimpse of the appearance of the Absolute.

> False absolutes rule over the soul which is no longer able to put them to flight through the image of the true. . . . In the realm of Moloch honest men lie and compassionate men tortue. And they really and truly believe that brother-murder will prepare the way for brotherhood! There appears to be no escape from the most evil of all idolatry.[9]

The Silence of God

The most terrible consequence of the eclipse is the silence of God—the loss of the sense of God's nearness. "It seems senseless to turn to Him who, if He is here, will not trouble Himself about us; it seems hopeless to penetrate to Him who may . . . perhaps be the soul of the universe but not our Father." When history appears to be empty of God, "with nowhere a beckoning of His finger," it is difficult for an individual and even more for a people to understand themselves as addressed by God. "The experience of concrete answerability recedes more and more . . . man unlearns taking the relationship between God and himself seriously in the dialogic sense." During such times the world seems to be irretrievably abandoned to the forces of tyranny. In the image of Psalm 82, the world is given over by God to judges who "judge unjustly" and "lift up the face of the wicked." This situation is nowhere more clearly described in modern literature than in the novels of Franz Kafka: "His unexpressed, ever-present theme," writes Buber, "is the remoteness of the judge, the remoteness of the lord of the castle, the hiddenness, the eclipse. . . ." Kafka describes the human world as given over to the meaningless government of a slovenly bureaucracy without possibility of appeal: "From the hopelessly strange Being who gave this world into their impure hands, no message of comfort or promise penetrates to us. He is, but he is not present."[10]

Buber's last statement on the "eclipse of God" points us to the narrow ridge between hope and despair, affirmation and denial. The eclipse can be described as a silence of God's, said Buber, "or rather, since I cannot conceive of any interruption of the divine revelation, a condition that works on us as a silence of God." It works on us that way not because the divine revelation is directly streaming toward us but because we sense the absence of God's presence, or, even more terrible, the presence of his absence. Buber stated:

These last years in a great searching and questioning, seized ever anew by the shudder of the now, I have arrived no further than that I now distinguish a revelation through the hiding of the face, a speaking through the silence. The eclipse of God can be seen with one's eyes, it will be seen.

He, however, who today knows nothing other to say than, "See there, it grows lights!" he leads into error.[11]

When asked by his friend Max Brod what hope was to be found in his novel *The Castle,* Franz Kafka responded, "Infinite hope—for God. Only none for ourselves." If this summation is not, in fact, true for Kafka himself, as I have tried to show in the Kafka section of *Problematic Rebel,* it is still less true of Buber. The narrow ridge that Buber walked between awareness of the eclipse and affirmation of trust is captured in a Hasidic tale of the great Kotzker Rebbe, a tale that stands in striking contrast to Kafka's *Castle*:

The Lord of the Castle

Rabbi Mendel once spoke to his hasidim about a certain parable in Midrash: How a man passed by a castle and, seeing it on fire and no one trying to put out the blaze, thought that this must be a castle without an owner, until the lord of the castle looked down on him and said: "I am the lord of the castle." When Rabbi Mendel said the words: "I am the lord of the castle," all those around him were struck with great reverence, for they all felt: "The castle is burning, but it has a lord."[12]

The Renewal of Trust

Can we discern a way in which we can move to quench the burning of the castle, to overcome the eclipse with a renewed and deepened existential trust? "It is just the

depth of the crisis that empowers us to hope," said Buber
in "Genuine Dialogue and the Possibilities of Peace," the
speech which he gave on the occasion of receiving the
Peace Prize of the German Book Trade in 1953. We can
only grasp the full strength of this hope if we bear in mind
the spirit in which Buber accepted this most controversial
prize:

> About a decade ago a considerable number of Germans—there
> must have been many thousands of them—under the indirect
> command of the German government and the direct command
> of its representatives, killed millions of my people in a sys-
> tematically prepared and executed procedure whose organ-
> ized cruelty cannot be compared with any previous historical
> event. I, who am one of those who remained alive, have only
> in a formal sense a common humanity with those who took
> part in this action. They have so radically transposed them-
> selves into a sphere of monstrous inhumanity inaccessible to
> my conception, that not even hatred, much less an overcom-
> ing of hatred, was able to arise in me. And what am I that I
> could here presume to "forgive"![13]

Buber pointed to others who did not investigate the ru-
mors because they did not want to become martyrs and to
some who did become martyrs in their opposition to Hitler's extermination of the Jews. And he pointed to the
German youth of today in some of whom he still saw the
possibility of the human as opposed to the antihuman. What
is most real of all, albeit moving secretly in the depths, said
Buber, is "the latent healing and salvation in the face of
impending ruin." This is the power of turning that radically changes the situation, the power that never reveals
itself outside of crisis. In its depths the crisis demands a
decision between the decomposition and the renewal of its
tissue. This turning, as Buber pointed out in "Prophecy,
Apocalyptic, and the Historical Hour" *(Pointing the Way),*

is "not a return to an earlier, guiltless stage of life, but a swinging round to where the wasted hither-and-thither becomes walking on a way, and guilt is atoned for in the newly-arisen genuineness of existence."

The crisis of mankind today announces itself most clearly as a crisis of trust. Bound up with this loss of trust in the closest possible fashion is the crisis of speech, "for I can only speak to someone in the true sense of the term if I expect him to accept my word as genuine. The fact that it is so difficult for present-day man to pray goes together with the fact that it is so difficult for him to carry on a genuine talk with his fellow men. This lack of trust in Being, this incapacity for unreserved intercourse with the other, points to an innermost sickness of the sense of existence." Despite this sickness and the "cold war" that was its symptom, Buber affirmed his belief that the peoples could enter into genuine dialogue with one another, that each, even in opposing the other, could heed, affirm, and confirm its opponent as an existing other. "Only so can conflict certainly not be eliminated from the world, but be humanly arbitrated and led towards its overcoming." Concluding "Genuine Dialogue and the Possibilities of Peace," Buber called on all of us not to let the Satanic element in men— the antihuman in individuals and in the human race—hinder us from realizing man. "Let us release speech from its ban! Let us dare, despite all, to trust!" "One cannot produce genuine dialogue, but one can be at its disposal," wrote Buber in "Prophecy, Apocalyptic, and the Historical Hour." "Existential mistrust cannot be replaced by trust, but it can be replaced by a reborn candour."

Only through this renewal of immediacy between person and person can we again experience immediacy in the dialogue with God. "When the man who has become solitary can no longer say 'Thou' to the 'dead' known God, everything depends on whether he can still say it to the living unknown God by saying 'thou' with all his being to another living and known man.'' If after long silence and stammering we genuinely say Thou to persons who are unlike ourselves and whom we recognize in all their otherness, then we shall have addressed our eternal Thou anew. Before we can genuinely address the eternal Thou, however, we must escape from that modern idolatry which leads us to sacrifice "the ethical" on the altar of our particular causes. A new conscience must arise in human beings which will summon them to guard with the innermost power of their souls against the confusion of the relative with the Absolute.

> To penetrate again and again into the false absolute with an incorruptible, probing glance until one has discovered its limits, its limitedness—there is today perhaps no other way to reawaken the power of the pupil to glimpse the never-vanishing appearance of the Absolute.[14]

We have to deal with the meaningless till the last moment, writes Buber in a comment on Franz Kafka, but in the very act of suffering its contradiction we experience an inner meaning. This meaning is not at all agreeable to us yet it is turned toward us, and it "pushes straight through all the foulness to the chambers of our hearts." Kafka depicted the course of the world in gloomier colors than ever before, yet he also proclaimed existential trust anew, "with a still deepened 'in spite of all this,' quite soft and shy, but unambiguous." So must existential trust change in a time of God's eclipse in order to persevere steadfast to God, without disowning reality. "By its very nature trust is substantiation of trust in the fulness of life in spite of the course of the world which is experienced." The eclipse of the light of God is no extinction. Although the I-Thou relation has gone into the catacombs, something is taking place in the depths that even tomorrow may bring it forth with new power.[15]

"To yield to seeming is man's essential cowardice, to resist it is his essential courage," wrote Buber in "Elements of the Interhuman" *(The Knowledge of Man).* Our need to be confirmed by one another itself leads to an essential corruption of the interhuman. Yet this is not an inexorable state of affairs. One can struggle to come to oneself, to come to confidence in being. "One must at times pay dearly for life lived from the being; but it is never too dear." In opposition to those who see bad weeds as growing everywhere, Buber asserted, "I have never known a young person who seemed to me irretrievably bad." Even in the grown person, when layer upon layer of seeming makes it seem like a fixed nature that cannot be overturned, the foreground is deceitful. "Man as man can be redeemed."

In this same essay Buber claims that by far the greater part of what is called conversation today is really speechifying in which persons do not speak to one another but "to a fictitious court of appeal whose life consists of nothing but listening to" them. In his play *The Cherry Orchard,* Chekhov depicted this situation as a deficiency of the person shut up in himself. But Sartre elevated this inability to communicate into an inevitable human destiny. Sartre's denial of the possibility of an essential relation between one person and another Buber labeled "the clearest expression of the wretched fatalism of modern man." In contrast to this fatalism, Buber gave clear expression to an existential trust shining through the darkness of the eclipse:

He who really knows how far our generation has lost the way of true freedom, of free giving between I and Thou, must himself, by virtue of the demand implicit in every great knowledge of this kind, practise directness—even if he were the only man on earth who did it—and not depart from it until scoffers are struck with fear, and hear in his voice the voice of their own suppressed longing.[16]

Appendix: Dialectical Faith versus Dialogical Trust
Response to Hopper's "Eclipse of God and Existential Mistrust"

Stanley Romaine Hopper's "Eclipse of God and Existential Mistrust"[1] is truly breathtaking in its brilliance of analysis and breadth of scope. I shall not undertake to do justice to it as a whole. Nor will I attempt to present a balanced valuation of it, such as is done by Thomas J.J. Altizer. I see my own special contribution, rather, as focussing on his interpretation of the thought of Martin Buber—a task for which Professor Hopper will grant my competence even where he differs with my stance.

Hopper recognizes that Buber would dispute his speaking of the "I-Thou relation" as a metaphor. Yet Hopper clearly does not understand from what standpoint Buber claims in *I and Thou* that "Thou" is not a metaphor. For Buber "Thou" is not a pronoun that stands for some noun, a linguistic symbol of some transcendent reality. It is the word of address that is spoken from within the relationship and that gives no information whatsoever concerning the nature and essence of one's partner in dialogue. When Hopper suggests that "Thou" is Buber's name for Tillich's God beyond "God" or for the "Transcendent," he reveals a fundamental misunderstanding of Buber's thought that necessarily impairs everything else he has to say on this subject. For Buber, religious symbols are symbols of the I-Thou relationship, not of God as he is in himself. Therefore the "Thou" is not, in fact, separable from the saying of "Thou" within an actual I-Thou relationship. It cannot refer to any designation of God, however transcendent and ineffable. Buber's "eternal Thou" is not a symbol of "God." "God," for Buber, is a symbol of the "eternal Thou," and the eternal Thou is the eternally renewed Thou of the concrete, particular I-Thou relationship.

Hopper seemingly reverses this position and takes seriously—as "another side" of Buber's teaching—a "certain literalism" which "invades this sense of the Mystery and coerces it towards the traditional dualistic models."

> His language continues to assert the terminological screen of "transcendence" and the "Absolute," of that which is "over against me," of "holding fast to the living God," of betweenness and encounter and of Pascal's "God of Abraham," phrases held not metaphorically or archetypally, but as he says, in a "real," "existential" and "actual" sense of which language as metaphor would somehow seem to deprive it.[2]

Actually, Hopper is making the same error as before, namely, imagining that the "Thou" of the I-Thou relationship refers by itself, apart from the relationship, to something outside of it. The only question for Hopper is whether that reference is properly couched in terms of metaphor so that it does not limit the ineffable reality of the Absolute, grounded in the depths of Jung's collective unconscious so that it may have "archetypal" significance without literal meaning, or whether it is taken as a literal, hence dualist referent. Buber rejects both of these possibilities in favor of the concreteness of the unique happening and event. If he does, indeed, espouse "betweenness" and "meeting" ("Encounter" is a translation for *Begegnung* that Buber did not like or use.), that is not because of any "literalness" of reference but the exact and true opposite—a meaning that cannot be divorced from the mutual knowing of dialogue.

While Hopper makes no secret of his preference for Heidegger over Buber, one is nonetheless astonished by the distortion that this preference introduces into his mere reporting of Buber's position. Accepting as his own Heidegger's goal of recovering for Western consciousness a "fundamental ontology," Hopper transmutes Buber's critique of Heidegger's concept of being into a concession. It gives evidence, Hopper claims, that "in the zones of ontological reflection Martin Buber's thinking remains enmeshed in the traditional rhetoric." Against all the evidence of everything that Buber has written, Hopper proceeds to conclude that Buber's "summation symbol, 'God,' often sounds like that which Wallace Stevens referred to as 'that Gold Self aloft, Alone . . . looking down," and hence untouched by what is most radical in the metaphors of 'death,' 'absence,' 'loss,' 'disappearance,' and even 'eclipse,' which terms . . . prevent our wishful return into that hermetic Eden of intellectualistically oriented thinking which has comprised the tradition of Western metaphysics from Aristotle down . . ." (page 50). I wish Buber were still alive to enjoy, as he truly would have, the spectacle of his thought being subsumed under the tradition of Western metaphysics!

What Buber actually writes is radically different from what Hopper reads through the lenses of his Heideggerian approach. In the context of a concise but thoroughgoing critique of Heidegger's teaching of the rebirth of divine images through man's concept-clarifying thought, Buber states:

> This is not the place for a critical discussion of Heidegger's theory of being. I shall only confess that for me a concept of being that means anything other than the inherent fact of all existing being, namely, that it exists, remains insurmountably empty. That is, unless I have recourse to religion and see in it a philosophical characterization of the Godhead similar to that of some Christian scholastics and mystics who contemplate, or think that they contemplate, the Godhead as it is in itself, thus as prior to creation. It should also be noted, however, that one of them, and the greatest of them all, Meister Eckhart, follows in Plato's footsteps by placing above the *esse est Deus,* as the higher truth, the sentence, *"Est enim (Deus) super esse et ens."* Compare this with Heidegger's statement (*Platons Lehre,* 76): " 'Being'—that is not God and it is not a ground of the world. Being is more than all that exists and is, nonetheless, nearer than any existing thing, be it . . . an angel or God. Being is the nearest thing." If by the last sentence, however, something other is meant that that I myself am, and not indeed as the subject of a *cogito,* but as my total person, then the concept of being loses for me the character of conceivability that obviously it eminently possesses for Heidegger.[3]

So also with Jung. Hopper's failure to notice Buber's critique of the psychologizing of reality makes him so misunderstand Buber's thesis that Jung has contributed to the "eclipse of God" as to convert this into the judgment that

Jung fits into the "God is dead" category. Neither did Buber ever suggest, as Hopper claims, that the unconscious is "an irrational function of my rational ego." Nor does Buber's carefully documented critique of Jung's relegating transcendence to a symbol of the psychologically immanent justify Hopper's characterization of Buber's aim as that of preserving the I-Thou relationship "in its externality," whatever that could possibly mean. What Buber has said is that those who confine God to the transcendent make him less than he is, but those who reduce him to the immanent mean something other than God. If this latter contributes, in Buber's opinion, to the "eclipse of God," it is not because he is attached to any dualistic transcendence, but because he is suspicious of a God reached by the removal of the otherness and uniqueness met in the "lived concrete."

From misunderstanding and misinterpretation Hopper proceeds to amateur psychoanalysis: "Buber's defensiveness arises from the sense of threat that he feels at the point where Jung's theory of the Unconscious subverts the classical model of a person, and thus, by extension threatens the adequacy of the 'I-Thou relation' model" (page 50). Although Hopper later discusses Buber's concept of "unmasking" from "Hope for This Hour" *(Pointing the Way),* he misses Buber's central point, namely, that the game of unmasking the motives of others quickly becomes mutual and leads to an existential mistrust that makes it impossible to attend to *what* the other says because one is so busy figuring out *why* he says it! Since Buber has made his critique of both Heidegger and Jung in great detail, with careful documentation, and with a full philosophical explanation of its significance, one might more easily ask what makes Hopper so defensive about Buber's criticism of his two intellectual heroes that he cannot grasp its plain intention. No one who has read *I and Thou* with any openness, much less

Buber's other works, could imagine that Buber is concerned with "the primacy of the rationalist ego," or "the person . . . deprived of its depth dimension," or "a mind in the body over against God and the world," or a "cerebral and assertive" dialogue as opposed to one that is "watchful and attentive" of "the creative *élan* that comes out of silence" (page 50). Such gross misreading betrays a dogmatism based on a very un-Zen-like dualism between "good" nondualistic terms and "bad" classical, dualistic, absolutistic, or intellectualist terms. From these dichotomies arises Hopper's evident inability to imagine that paradoxical combination of transcendence and immanence that lies at the heart of Buber's philosophy and, in different form, of Zen Buddhism.

Hopper mistrusts Buber's view of mistrust as not sufficiently radical. But when he deals with that unmasking of which Buber speaks in connection with Marx, Nietzsche, and Freud, he entirely misses the distortion that existential mistrust inevitably brings in its wake—the belief that one has ideas and ideals while the other has only rationalizations and ideologies, to be seen through and reinterpreted but never to be taken as a valid expression of a really other point of view. On the contrary, Hopper sees "unmasking" only as a positive phenomenon which strips off pretensions and presumptions and confronts "us with the primary mysteries of being and self-identity," releasing us "into a fresh understanding of the nature and 'meaning' of things."

Hopper sees his thought as new and more radical than Buber's, whereas I see Hopper's position as an up-to-date essentialism of a traditional Western or Hindu metaphysical nature, without a trace of existential anguish. This may account, in part, for his total failure to grasp the fundamental issues of ontology between Heidegger and Buber. He equates "Buber's existential relations" with Heidegger's "entities" as elements for which we lack the grammar that would enable us to grasp them in their Being (page 54). He thus reduces Buber's sphere of the between to the "ontic," the merely existential, and accords to Heidegger's hypostasized non-relational Being the sole conceivable ontological reality. But Buber has said repeatedly and in all clarity that to him it is the "between" itself that is the "ontological," and he has denied the possibility of reaching any "Being" through plumbing the depths of the self or even as the ground of self and world.

When Hopper deals with Buber's interpretation of the Heraclitean "logos" in "What Is Common to All" *(The Knowledge of Man),* he again ignores the real issue between Buber and Heidegger—whether "man" may bring about the "unconcealment of Being" directly or only through the "between," i.e., in that common "speech-with-meaning" *(logos)* through which he builds a common cosmos. Instead Hopper claims that Buber's use of the term *logos* "tends to function rationalistically, losing its ratios of physical depth and losing its thrust as one metaphor in a cluster of vitalistic metaphors which, taken together, convey something of Heraclitus' vision of things." But Buber *has* used Heraclitus' *logos* in the context of an interpretation of his "vitalistic metaphors and figurations of the unity of opposites." The very term "unity of opposites" figures centrally in Buber's own thought from his 1901 essay on Jacob Boehme, his 1904 dissertation on Nicolas of Cusa and Jacob Boehme, his 1911 essay on "The Teaching of the Tao," his 1913 chapter on "Polarity" in *Daniel* to, and through, the whole of his mature thought. "The unity of the contraries is the mystery at the innermost core of the dialogue," Buber himself wrote. Not only has Hopper merely put Heidegger forward in place of Buber without facing the issue between them, he has missed the heart of Buber's philosophy—the *coincidentia oppositorum.*

Hopper finds the figural terms of Buber's metaphor of

"eclipse" "not radical enough to embrace the paradoxical sense of desolation and release which we today experience." But has Hopper really experienced the desolation that arises, not out of some Socratic, Kierkegaardian, or Nietzschean dialectic, but out of the "hiding of God" in the time of Auschwitz? Does he understand Buber's refusal in the name of "the Job of Auschwitz" to put up with earthly being, his insistence on struggling for its redemption, and his readiness to meet, in whatever form he comes, "our cruel and kind Lord who is again and still a hiding one"? Has Hopper even asked himself what commentary Heidegger's Naziism throws on his attempt to unconceal Being minus genuine dialogue with real otherness? Hopper locates "the *place* where the seeming contradictions of theophany and reversal are occurring" as "contemporary literature" which "*embodies* the enigma that it seeks to solve." In so doing he is in danger of elevating literature to a sphere above life. If there is a "new myth that is forming at the heart of the world," then we cannot look for its first signs in literature and art alone, as Hopper suggests, but in the full historical reality, including that Dialogue with the Absurd (to use my own terminology) that is the only stance that does not evade those historical contradictions that we cannot make meaningful either within a rational world-view or a mystic insight into the heart of things.

When Hopper himself comes to discussing the "death of God," we are confirmed in what we already suspected: the parochial framework of his system of denials. He equates "God's failure" with that "recession of Christendom's symbolic system, along with the classical world-view," which "renders everything uncertain." No wonder that he cannot understand the non-Christian and non-Greek nature of Buber's thought. What Hopper is really talking about is a chapter in the intellectual history of the Western world rather than those holocausts and abysses of modern history that have put man himself in question.

The goal of Hopper's paper, as he states it, is "to accomplish the negative and to focus our uncertainty infinitely in order that the Deity, the positive, that which is already given, might be glimpsed through his creative Presence." This Kierkegaardian type of dialectic is full of intellectual paradoxes, but it misses the genuinely existential and historical ones. Put in another way, it is the difference between "dialectic" and "dialogue." Dialectic, whether it is seen as individual reasoning or the sweep of world-historical consciousness à la Hegel, is essentially monological. In its perspective, existential mistrust and the failure of dialogue does not really threaten contact with reality, but in the end serves to promote it. Hence even in its progression of opposites and its radical negations and affirmations, it is still an essentialist approach. For the life of dialogue, in contrast, the existential mistrust that results from and exacerbates the failure of dialogue cannot be overcome intellectually or dialectically but only through an event of new meeting—through a renewal of trust that comes, if at all, only out of an honest facing of existential contradictions.

In his last statement on the "eclipse of God," Buber pointed out that its divine side is what the Hebrew Bible speaks of as "the hiding of God." This is an event *between* God and man rather than something that in any way breaks off the divine revelation, but it is a real event that no dialectic can conjure away:

> One may also call what is meant here a silence of God's or rather, since I cannot conceive of any interruption of the divine revelation, a condition that works on us as a silence of God. One is right to see here a "most troubling question." These last years in a great searching and questioning, seized ever anew by the shudder of the now, I have arrived no fur-

ther than that I now distinguish a revelation through the hiding of the face, a speaking through the silence. The eclipse of God can be seen with one's eyes, it will be seen.

He, however, who today knows nothing other to say than, "See there, it grows lighter!" he leads into error.[4]

Dialectic, for all its dynamism, is still bound to the subject-object way of knowing—the very dimension that Hopper imagines he has transcended. After his progress through Heidegger, Jung, Wallace Stevens, Zen, and so much else, Hopper ends with Rilke, or more exactly with Rilke interpreted in a subjective-objective duality that Rilke himself overcame in his *Duino Elegies*:

Rilke proposed that perhaps we have made a mistake in trying to look *at* God, thus making an object of him, standing over against us; perhaps we ought, as he said, to see as God sees— in which case, God would be behind us, so to speak, like the enigma *a priori,* and we would be looking in the same direction as he is looking, seeing as he sees, participating, that is, in his creative life, even as the poet today strives to be one with his poem, participating thereby in the ontology of utterance, provided of course that the utterance comes from a psychical source deeper than the cavern beneath his inmost cave.[5]

In *The Knowledge of Man,* both in "What Is Common to All" and in "The Word That Is Spoken," Buber put forward an "ontology of utterance" based squarely on the reality of the life *between* man and man. But Hopper totally misses this, even as a theoretical possibility, just as he misses Buber's distinction between existence as *Gegenüber* or *Gegenstand* ("vis-à-vis" or "object") when he speaks of God as "an object . . . standing over against us." Hopper only knows God as object or as subject.

The third alternative, of a God who is met in the "between," i.e. in the meeting with the nameless Meeter, but not in any knowledge of some "object," is simply left out. When Hopper wants to go beyond the merely personal, he falls into that archetypal psychologizing of God and existence evident in his referring the "ontology of utterance" to a "psychological source" more profound than the individual himself. What troubles me most of all in Hopper's stance is not the religious dimension per se, but the human. In turning away from the meeting with what transcends the self to the Self alone, he does not do justice to the lived reality of existence itself, which does not take place within the psyche, no matter how profoundly conceived. Against Hopper I repeat what I wrote at the end of my Introductory Essay to *The Knowledge of Man*: "Martin Buber's philosophical anthropology refers us with a profundity unequalled in our time to man's still unfathomed relation to being and meaning."[6]

Reference Notes

PREFACE

1. Maurice Friedman, *Martin Buber's Life and Work: The Early Years—1878-1923* (New York: E. P. Dutton, 1982); *The Middle Years—1923-1945* (New York: E. P. Dutton, 1983); *The Later Years—1945-1965* (New York: E. P. Dutton, 1984).
2. Maurice Friedman, *The Human Way: A Dialogical Approach to Religion and Human Experience* (Chambersburg, Pa.: Anima Publications, 1982).
3. Maurice Friedman, *"You Are My Witnesses": Abraham Joshua Heschel and Elie Wiesel* (New York: Farrar, Straus & Giroux, 1986).

CHAPTER 1

1. Martin Buber, *Eclipse of God: Studies in the Relation between Religion and Philosophy* (New York: Harper Torchbooks, 1957), Chapter 3, "Religion and Philosophy," trans. by Maurice S. Friedman, p. 35f.
2. *Ibid.,* p. 44f.

3. Martin Buber, *Pointing the Way: Collected Essays,* ed. & trans. by Maurice Friedman (New York: Schocken Books, 1974), "Goethe's Concept of Humanity," p. 79.
4. *Eclipse of God,* "Religion and Philosophy," p. 45.
5. Martin Buber, *Between Man and Man,* trans. by Ronald Gregor Smith, with an Introduction by Maurice Friedman (New York: Macmillan, 1965), "The Education of Character," p. 114.
6. Martin Buber, *Good and Evil: Two Interpretations* (New York: Charles Scribner's Sons, 1953), p. 142.

CHAPTER 2

1. Maurice S. Friedman, *Martin Buber: The Life of Dialogue,* 3rd ed. with a new Preface and an expanded Bibliography (Chicago and London: The University of Chicago Press, 1976), pp. vi, 33.
2. Martin Buber, *Ich und Du* (Heidelberg: Verlag Lambert Schneider, 1974), Part Three, p. 99, trans. by Maurice Friedman. See also "Nachwort," p. 116.
3. *Between Man and Man,* "The Question to the Single One," p. 52.
4. *Ibid.,* "Education," p. 94f.
5. *Ibid.,* p. 102.
6. Friedman, *Martin Buber: The Life of Dialogue,* p. 170.
7. Martin Buber, *On Judaism,* ed. by Nahum N. Glatzer (New York: Schocken Books, 1968, paperback, 1972), "The Dialogue between Heaven and Earth" (1952), pp. 214-16.
8. Martin Buber, *Israel and the World: Essays in a Time of Crisis* (New York: Schocken Books, 1963), "The Man of Today and the Jewish Bible," p. 93.
9. *Israel and the World,* "The Two Foci of the Jewish Soul," p. 34f.
10. *Ibid.,* "The Faith of Judaism," p. 26.
11. The above sections on "Turning and Redemption" and "Sacramental Existence" are based on Friedman, *Martin Buber: The Life of Dialogue,* Chap. 17—"The Redemption of Evil," pp. 133–48, where the reader will also find the exact sources.

12. Julius Guttmann, *Philosophies of Judaism,* trans. by David W. Silverman, Introduction by R. J. Zwi Werblowsky (New York: Holt, Rinehart, & Winston, 1964), p. ix.

Chapter 3

1. Paul Arthur Schilpp and Maurice Friedman, eds., *The Philosophy of Martin Buber,* Volume XII of The Library of Living Philosophers (LaSalle, Illinois: The Open Court Publishing Co., London: Cambridge University Press, 1967), Martin Buber, "Replies to My Critics," trans. by Maurice Friedman, p. 690.
2. Sydney and Beatrice Rome, eds., *Philosophical Interrogations* (New York: Harper Torchbooks, 1970), "Martin Buber" section, conducted, edited, and trans. by Maurice Friedman, p. 53f.
3. *Ibid.,* p. 53f.
4. Schilpp and Friedman, eds., *The Philosophy of Martin Buber,* p. 705.
5. Rome and Rome, eds., *Philosophical Interrogations,* p. 84.
6. Schilpp and Friedman, eds., *The Philosophy of Martin Buber,* p. 690.
7. *Ich und Du, loc. cit.,* Part Three, p. 97.
8. See *The Philosophy of Martin Buber,* pp. 49–68, 717.
9. See Ronald W. Hepburn, *Christianity and Paradox: Critical Studies in Twentieth Century Theology* (London: Watts, 1966; New York: Pegasus, 1968); C. B. Martin, "A Religious Way of Knowing" in Antony Flew and Alisdair McIntyre, eds., *New Essays in Philosophical Theology* (New York: Macmillan, 1955), pp. 76–95.
10. Martin Buber, *A Believing Humanism: Gleanings,* trans., with an Introduction and Explanatory Comments by Maurice Friedman (New York: Simon & Schuster, 1968), p. 113.
11. *Ibid.,* p. 132.
12. *Ibid.,* p. 22.
13. Schilpp and Friedman, eds., *The Philosophy of Martin Buber,* p. 696f.
14. *A Believing Humanism,* p. 135.

CHAPTER 4

1. As I have done in Chapter 22—"Ethics," in my book *Martin Buber: The Life of Dialogue.*
2. *Eclipse of God,* "Religion and Ethics," trans. by Maurice Friedman, p. 95.
3. Martin Buber, *The Knowledge of Man: A Philosophy of the Interhuman,* ed. with an Introductory Essay (Chap. 1) by Maurice Friedman (New York: Harper Torchbooks, 1966), "Distance and Relation," trans. by R. G. Smith, pp. 67 f., 71.
4. *Between Man and Man,* pp. 202–205; *The Knowledge of Man,* "Elements of the Interhuman," trans. by R. G. Smith, pp. 72–75.
5. *Between Man and Man,* pp. 20–24, 27, 29f., 36–39, 96f.; *The Knowledge of Man,* pp. 79–81.
6. *Between Man and Man,* pp. 61–69; letter of August 18, 1952 from Professor Buber to writer.
7. *Eclipse of God,* "Religion and Modern Thinking," trans. by Maurice S. Friedman, p. 87.
8. *Good and Evil,* "Images of Good and Evil," trans. by Michael Bullock, pp. 127, 140–143; *Between Man and Man,* p. 78 f.
9. *Good and Evil,* pp. 125–32, 139 f.
10. *Eclipse of God,* "Religion and Modern Thinking," p. 70.
11. *The Knowledge of Man,* "Elements of the Interhuman," p. 84.
12. *Between Man and Man,* p. 16.
13. *Ibid.,* p. 114.
14. *Eclipse of God,* "Religion and Ethics," p. 98.
15. *Good and Evil,* p. 143 f.
16. *Ich und Du,* Part Three, p. 137f; *Israel and the World,* p. 94f.
17. From a statement on revelation written by Buber in the fall of 1955 in response to questions of the present writer.
18. Or rather, as Buber himself puts it in response to this passage, in a letter to the present writer of October 7, 1958, "The first is necessarily my point of departure, the second is my hope that, as history tells me, can be fulfilled."

19. Martin Buber, *Hasidism and Modern Man,* ed. & trans. with an Introduction by Maurice Friedman (New York: Horizon Books, 1958), pp. 227–229, 232.
20. *Eclipse of God,* "On the Suspension of the Ethical," trans. by Maurice Friedman, p. 118.
21. *Ibid.,* p. 119f.

CHAPTER 5

1. *The Knowledge of Man,* "What is Common to All," trans. by Maurice Friedman, p. 100.
2. *Ibid.,* p. 107f.
3. *Ibid.,* p. 108f.
4. *The Knowledge of Man,* "Guilt and Guilt Feelings," trans. by Maurice Friedman, pp. 125 f., 132–136.
5. *Ibid.,* pp. 146–148.
6. *Ibid.,* p. 148.
7. *The Knowledge of Man,* "Elements of the Interhuman," p. 85.
8. *Between Man and Man,* pp. 36ff.; *Pointing the Way,* p. 206.
9. *Between Man and Man,* p. 17.
10. *The Knowledge of Man,* "Guilt and Guilt Feelings," pp. 125–127, 136.
11. *Ich und Du,* Part Three, p. 127.
12. *Ibid.,* p. 119.
13. From a letter to the author of October 7, 1958.
14. *Pointing the Way,* pp. 224, 229.
15. *Eclipse of God,* p. 68f.
16. Cf. Paul E. Pfuetze, *The Social Self* (New York: Bookmans Associates, 1954), pp. 280f., 296n, 152.
17. *Good and Evil,* "Right and Wrong," p. 54f.

CHAPTER 6

1. G. G. Van der Leeuw, *Religion in Essence and Manifestation: A Study in Phenomenology,* Vol. I, trans. by J. E. Turner (New York: Harper Torchbooks, 1963), "Author's Note to the English Edition" (1937), p. vi.

2. Martin Buber, *The Prophetic Faith,* trans. from the Hebrew by Carlyle Witton-Davies (New York: Harper Torchbooks, 1960), "Introduction," p. 6.

3. Martin Buber, *Two Types of Faith,* trans. by Norman P. Goldhawk (New York: Harper Torchbooks, 1961), Foreword, pp. 6–12.

4. Martin Buber, *The Origin and Meaning of Hasidism,* ed. and trans. with an Introduction by Maurice Friedman (New York: Horizon Press, 1973), "Supplement: Christ, Hasidism, Gnosis," p. 242f.

5. Schalom Ben-Chorin, *Zwiesprache mit Martin Buber, Ein Errinerungsbuch* (Munich: List Verlag, 1966), p. 183 f.; Walter Nigg, "Die drei Stationen Martin Bubers. Eine Würdigung" in Westdeutscher Rundfunk (Köln), III Program, September 29, 1962, p. 38f.

6. *A Believing Humanism,* "Fragments on Revelation," #3; "The Exclusive Attitude of the Religions," p. 115f.

7. *Ibid.,* "On the Science of Religion," pp. 127–129.

8. *The Origin and Meaning of Hasidism,* "God and the Soul," pp. 184–199.

9. *Ibid.,* "The Place of Hasidism in the History of Religion," pp. 220–239.

10. Martin Buber, *The Kingship of God,* 3rd., newly enlarged ed., trans. by Richard Scheimann (New York: Harper Torchbooks, 1973), "Preface to the First Edition," p. 18 f., "Preface to the Second Edition," p. 21 f.

11. *Ibid.,* "Preface to the Second Edition," p. 26 f.

12. *Ibid.,* "Preface to the Third Edition," pp. 47–52.

13. *Ibid.,* p. 56, Chap. 3, p. 85 f.

14. *Ibid.,* Chap. 7, pp. 121–123, Chap. 6, p. 119.

15. *Ibid.,* Chap. 5, p. 99.

16. Martin Buber, *Moses: The Revelation and the Covenant* (New York: Harper Torchbooks, 1958), "Preface," p. 7 f.

17. *Ibid.,* pp. 64, 136, 158.

18. *The Kingship of God,* "Preface to the Second Edition," p. 35 f.; *Moses,* pp. 78 f., 127.

19. *Moses,* p. 158.

CHAPTER 7

1. Martin Buber, *Der Jude und sein Judentum: Gesammelte Aufsätze und Reden* (Cologne: Joseph Melzer Verlag, 1963). "Herzl vor der Palastina-Karte (Aus meinen Errinerungen, 1944)," pp. 804–807.

2. Maurice Friedman, "Martin Buber's Encounter with Mysticism," *Human Inquiries: Review of Existential Psychology and Psychiatry*, Vol. X, 1970, pp. 43–81.

3. *Pointing the Way*, "The Teaching of the Tao," p. 48.

4. Thomas Merton, *The Way of Chuang-Tzu* (New York: New Directions, 1965), "The Woodcarver," p. 110f.

5. *Pointing the Way*, pp. 121–125.

6. Martin Buber, *Ereignisse und Begegnungen* (Leipzig: Insel Verlag, 1917), "Buddha," pp. 3–9.

7. *Ich und Du*, Part Three, pp. 108–111.

8. *Eclipse of God*, "Religion and Philosophy," p. 27f.

9. *The Origin and Meaning of Hasidism*, pp. 231–239.

10. Gershom Scholem, *The Messianic Idea in Judaism* (New York: Schocken Books, 1971), "Martin Buber's Interpretation of Hasidism," trans. by Michael A. Meyer, pp. 227–250.

11. For a full-scale discussion of this issue see Maurice Friedman, *Martin Buber's Life and Work: The Later Years— 1945–1965*, Chap. 12—"The Interpretation of Hasidism: Buber versus Scholem," pp. 280–299. See also Schilpp and Friedman, eds., *The Philosophy of Martin Buber*, Rivka Schatz-Uffenheimer, "Man's Relation to God and World in Buber's Rendering of the Hasidic Teaching," pp. 403–434; Buber, "Replies to My Critics, IX: On Hasidism," pp. 731–741; Martin Buber, "Interpreting Hasidism," trans. by Maurice Friedman, *Commentary*, Vol. XXXVI, No. 3 (September 1963), pp. 218–225. See Martin Buber, *Werke, III— Schriften zum Chassidismus* (Munich and Heidelberg: Kösel and Lambert Schneider Verlag, 1963), "Noche einiges zur Darstellung des Chassidismus," pp. 991–998.

12. The passages on Zen above and below are based on Maurice

Friedman, *Touchstones of Reality: Existential Trust and the Covenant of Peace* (New York: E. P. Dutton, 1972, and Dutton Books, 1974), Chap. 6—"Journey to the East," pp. 109–115.

13. *The Knowledge of Man*, "Elements of the Interhuman," p. 80f.
14. Martin Buber, *Tales of the Hasidim: The Later Masters*, trans. by Olga Marx (New York: Schocken Books, 1961), "Everywhere," p. 170.

CHAPTER 8

1. *A Believing Humanism*, "Religious Education," p. 126.
2. *Eclipse of God*, "Prelude: Report on Two Talks," trans. by Maurice Friedman, pp. 3–6.
3. *Ibid.*, pp. 6–9.
4. *Between Man and Man*, "Education," pp. 88–93.
5. *Israel and the World*, "The Man of Today and the Jewish Bible," pp. 90–96.
6. *Ibid.*, "Teaching and Deed," p. 140 f.; "Hebrew Humanism," p. 247.
7. *Between Man and Man*, "Education," p. 102 f.
8. *Eclipse of God*, "Religion and Reality," trans. by Norbert Guterman, pp. 13 f., 18 f., 23 f.; "Religion and Modern Thinking," p. 68 f.; "On the Suspension of the Ethical," p. 119; "God and the Spirit of Man," trans. by Maurice Friedman, pp. 127–129.
9. *Ibid.*, "God and the Spirit of Man," pp. 125–127.
10. *Israel and the World*, "Teaching and Deed," p. 139–145.
11. *Ibid.*, "On National Education," p. 161 f.
12. *Ibid.*, p. 162 f.
13. Martin Buber, *Tales of the Hasidim: The Early Masters*, trans. by Olga Marx (New York: Schocken Books, 1962), "Suffering and Prayer," p. 212 f.

CHAPTER 9

1. Sydney and Beatrice Rome, eds., *Philosophical Interroga-*

tions, Martin Buber VI: "The Bible and Biblical Judaism," p. 99f.

2. *On Judaism,* "The Biblical Dialogue between Heaven and Earth," p. 225.

3. Martin Buber, *Pointing the Way: Collected Essays,* ed. & trans. by Maurice Friedman (New York: Harper Bros., 1957), "Hope for This Hour," p. 224.

4. *Eclipse of God,* "Supplement: Reply to C. G. Jung," trans. by Maurice Friedman, p. 136.

5. *Ibid.,* "Religion and Modern Thinking," trans. by Maurice Friedman, p. 86.

6. *Ibid.,* pp. 70–77.

7. *Pointing the Way,* "The Validity and Limitation of the Political Principle," p. 215.

8. *Eclipse of God,* "God and the Spirit of Man," trans. by Maurice Friedman, p. 129.

9. *Ibid.,* "On the Suspension of the Ethical," trans. by Maurice Friedman, p. 119 f.

10. Martin Buber, *Two Types of Faith: A Study of the Interpenetration of Judaism and Christianity,* trans. by Norman P. Goldhawk (New York: Harper Torchbooks, 1961), pp. 162–169.

11. Schilpp and Friedman, eds., *The Philosophy of Martin Buber,* Martin Buber, "Replies to My Critics," trans. by Maurice Friedman, p. 716.

12. *Tales of the Hasidim: The Later Masters,* p. 275.

13. *Pointing the Way,* "Genuine Dialogue and the Possibilities of Peace," p. 120.

14. *Eclipse of God,* "On the Suspension of the Ethical," p. 120.

15. *Ibid.,* "God and the Spirit of Man," p. 129.

16. *The Knowledge of Man,* "Elements of the Interhuman," p. 79.

APPENDIX

1. *The Eastern Buddhist,* New Series, Vol. IV, No. 1, May 1971. Originally this was a lecture at a Conference on Religion & Literature at Temple University in December 1969. I

suggested this title to Professor Hopper never dreaming he would focus on Buber. The conference was sponsored by the Ph.D. program in Religion and Literature which I directed.
2. *Ibid.*, p. 49.
3. *Eclipse of God,* "Religion and Modern Thinking," p. 73 f.
4. Schilpp and Friedman, eds., *The Philosophy of Martin Buber,* Martin Buber, "Replies to My Critics," p. 716.
5. Hopper, "Eclipse of God and Existential Mistrust," p. 69.
6. *The Knowledge of Man,* p. 58.

Index